A CELEBRATION OF SOUPS

Books by Robert Ackart

THE HUNDRED MENU CHICKEN COOKBOOK

COOKING IN A CASSEROLE

FRUITS IN COOKING

THE ONE-DISH COOKBOOK

A CELEBRATION OF VEGETABLES

THE CHEESE COOKBOOK

SOUFFLES, MOUSSES, JELLIES, AND CREAMS

A CELEBRATION OF SOUPS

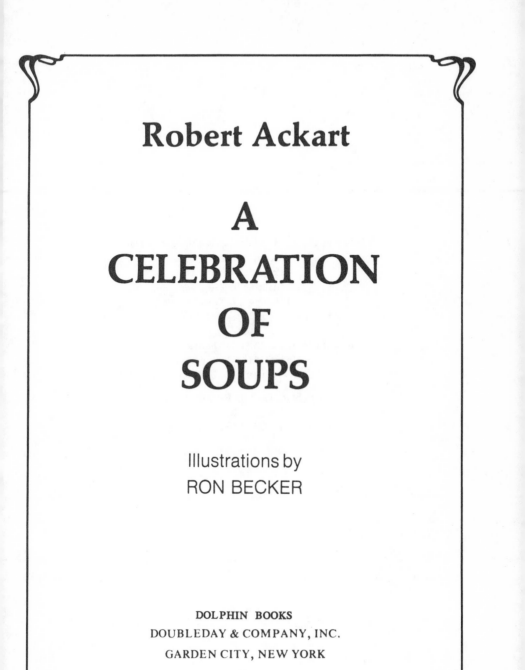

Robert Ackart

A
CELEBRATION
OF
SOUPS

Illustrations by
RON BECKER

DOLPHIN BOOKS
DOUBLEDAY & COMPANY, INC.
GARDEN CITY, NEW YORK

1982

Library of Congress Cataloging in Publication Data
Ackart, Robert C.
A celebration of soups.
Includes index.
1. Soups.   I. Title.
TX757.A24   641.8'13
AACR2
ISBN: 0-385-15847-5 (hardcover)
ISBN: 0-385-18141-8 (paperback)
Library of Congress Catalog Card Number 81–43248

BOOK DESIGN BY BENTE HAMANN

First Edition

For

Marion and Barton G. Hocker

Contents

Introduction

Everybody loves soup!

It is universally popular. It is man's earliest made dish and, having played an important role in nourishing us through eons of becoming civilized, it appeals to us as a fundamental food. We are molded by habit to like it. It is part of us.

Soup is comfortable. Because it has been cooked long and slowly, it is friendly to even the most delicate digestion. Soup is soothing; in winter, its homely earthiness communicates to us so that we are warmed by it, physically and emotionally; in summer, a refreshing chilled or jellied soup makes us feel cooler and happily fed.

Soup is a sociable dish; as an attractive first course, it stimulates our appetite without slaking it, encourages fellowship at the dining table, and heightens our expectations of what foods will follow; as a main dish capable of hundreds of guises, it leaves us satisfied, but with no feeling of heaviness.

Soup-making, a cooking accomplishment of high order, is considered by some to be the cook's ultimate achievement. And it is, from the cook's viewpoint, virtually effortless, for the greater part of the work is done, unattended, in the simmering kettle.

Soup-making is kind to the family budget, a fact especially true of many main-course soups using vegetables and spare or leftover meats. True, soup-making *can* be rather elegantly extravagant—if you want to splurge on a first-course oyster bisque, for example. But for everyday meals soup is without competition as low-priced fare.

This book is the result of trial and error in soup-making, of inventing soups, of altering existing recipes to suit my whim or taste or purpose. It is a personal book, reflecting my likes and, by omission, my dislikes. It is a book about soups for the love of them, the pleasure you will have in making them, and the satisfaction they will afford at the table. Underlying these *desiderata* is a design which I hope will facilitate your making the soup of your choice.

The book embraces: hot thick soups—which can be a meal in themselves—of meat, poultry, fish, legumes (dried beans, peas, etc.), and vegetables; thin (which include clear) soups; chilled and jellied soups; hot and chilled cream and cream-style soups; cheese-based soups; and hot and chilled fruit and nut soups.

Because the organization of the book is by types of soups, principal ingredients are scattered throughout. Recipes for fish and seafood, for example, appear in the section devoted to cream and cream-style soups in addition to those in the Fish Soups section; fruits are found in the hot thick soup category as well as in the Hot and Cold Fruit and Nut Soups section; Chicken Stock, that most used of all soup-making liquids, appears everywhere—and so forth. Because the categories as listed in the Contents frequently overlap, the Index is designed to cross-reference all recipes so that they may be easily found.

If a soup is typical of a particular national cuisine, the country from which it comes is identified. There are only a few Chinese and Japanese soups, regretfully; the most typical ones must be absolutely clear, a fact increasing the cook's effort, and, more importantly, many of their ingredients are generally unavailable save in large metropolitan areas. Those which I do offer are typical of these delectable cuisines, but present no particular problem in the acquisition of their ingredients. Sometimes I give a personal comment on the recipe in order to pique your curiosity and appetite and to share with you my enthusiasms. Those soups which to my best knowledge are of my creation are indicated by an asterisk (*). Recipes whose titles are capitalized can be found by consulting the Index.

The approximate preparation time, appearing at the head of each recipe, does not include standing, drying, or chilling time. All ingredients are listed in order of their use; the procedures applicable to these ingredients appear in the column parallel to them. Unless otherwise stated, fresh vegetables are used. The approximate yield of each recipe is indicated. If desired, the recipes may be doubled. They may be refrigerated or frozen. All measurements for herbs are for dried herbs unless otherwise indicated. (Please read the introductory section, "Note on the Terms Used in This Book," wherein such technical material is dealt with specifically.)

Come with me now to the kitchen where together we will make appealing, delicious, satisfying soups!

ROBERT ACKART
Katonah, New York
1981

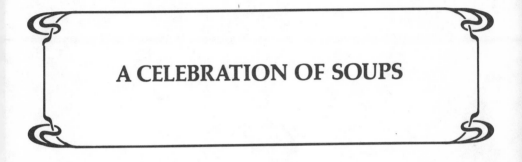

A CELEBRATION OF SOUPS

NOTE ON THE TERMS
USED IN THIS BOOK

The following section is important to the use of this book; I hope you will read it. For your convenience the subjects are entered alphabetically and cross-referenced when necessary. The material provides definitions for terms used in the recipes, such as beurre manié *and* roux, *for example— French expressions which say so exactly what they mean that we have adopted them. Many of the entries deal with "how to"—how to defat soup or homogenize a thawed frozen one, for example. Although I am aware that cooks want to get into recipes right off (I do myself), I believe you will enjoy using this book more and find the preparation of the soups easier if you have read this section before setting out.*

Beer: a fine addition to cabbage, legume, and hearty vegetable soups. Add 1 cupful of warm, stale beer to 3 or 4 cupfuls of soup; do not allow the soup to return to the boil.

Blender (see Processor)

Bouquet garni: a selection of herbs and spices used to season stock and broth and discarded upon completion of the cooking. To facilitate their removal, tie fresh herbs together with string; such seasonings as whole cloves, peppercorns, and dried herbs are easily discarded if you tie them in a bit of cheesecloth or put them in a metal tea ball with screw-on top. There are various *bouquets garnis,* but three I find especially useful (to flavor 8 cupfuls of liquid)— Number one: 2 bay leaves, 2 whole cloves, 1 clove of garlic, peeled and split, 8 sprigs of parsley, 6 peppercorns, ½ teaspoonful of thyme. Number two: 3 bay leaves, 4 celery tops with leaves, 3 whole cloves, ½ teaspoonful of marjoram, 8 sprigs of parsley, 8 peppercorns, ½ teaspoonful of summer savory, ½ teaspoonful of thyme. Number three: 2 bay leaves, 3 celery tops with leaves, ½ teaspoonful of marjoram, 4 sprigs of parsley, 1 teaspoonful of sage, 1 teaspoonful of summer savory. For fish soups, add to this last *bouquet garni* a 4- or 5-inch piece of orange zest and, if desired, a few leaves of rosemary.

Canned broth: given in these recipes as an alternate to homemade stock, canned broth produces a very acceptable soup. The size of can called for in all recipes is the 10½-ounce tin. If you wish to defat canned broth (as I always do), place the can in the refrigerator overnight and, when ready to use the broth, open the can and pour the liquid through a strainer; the fat will have congealed and is easily discarded.

Cheese: for garnish take a little extra trouble and grate the fresh cheese yourself. This nicety can be accomplished easily in the container of a food processor (use the steel knife). The difference in flavor between your fresh-grated cheese and the supermarket's packaged brand is wide indeed.

Chilling time: convinced that a chilled soup should be truly chilled and that a jellied one should be thoroughly gelled, I recommend 4 hours in the refrigerator for chilled soups (after the recipe has cooled to room temperature) and 6 hours for jellied soups (once again, after the recipe has cooled to room temperature). As a general rule, it is best to adjust the seasoning of a chilled soup *after* it has been chilled.

Cooling soup: do so as quickly as possible, by removing the lid from the saucepan or soup kettle, so that solid ingredients do not continue to cook in the hot liquid. Refrigerate soups only when they have reached room temperature.

Cream: in the recipes I recommend light or heavy cream, whichever seems best to fit the purposes at hand. If, however, you want a richer soup, do not hesitate to use heavy cream, or if you prefer a lower calorie count, use light cream—or half-and-half. Incidentally, in cream and cream-style soups, powdered milk may always be added for extra protein, but very few extra calories. Scalding cream (and milk) tends to reduce the chances of its curdling when added to the other ingredients; for this reason, I sometimes suggest doing so, especially if the mixture of other ingredients is acid. There is no need for scalding (see page 5) when cream (or milk) is added to bland mixtures.

Defatting soups: soups with a layer of hot grease floating on top of them are not very attractive to look at, and if consumed are most certainly unkind to the waistline. Both pitfalls can be easily avoided by any one of three measures. Method one is my favorite because it is easiest and surest: allow the soup or stock or mixture you wish to defat to come fully to room temperature; refrigerate it overnight, during which time the fat will solidify; the next day, remove and discard it—simple as that. Method two: gently float a paper towel on the surface of the liquid and discard it (the hot fat, lighter than the soup liquid, will rise to the top); repeat as necessary until the fat has been removed—this is a good way to remove fat from soups made in smallish quantity. Method three: use a meat baster with a rubber bulb as a suction device to draw up the liquid fat and collect it in a can or jar; in my estimation, this is the least successful method, as you will inevitably lose some of the soup itself. (To defat canned broth, see Canned Broth, page 2).

Fish: unless otherwise indicated, I rely on fresh lean white-fleshed fish fillets (cod, flounder, haddock, halibut, scrod, or sole). They come from the fishmonger clean and ready to use. Their flavor is at once delicate and full. If it is more convenient to use frozen fish, by all means do so. Allow it to thaw partially before adding it to the soup kettle.

Freezing: the recipes may be frozen for future use. When a frozen soup is to be served, allow it to thaw fully to room temperature. Stock-based soups should be heated gently and served promptly to prevent such ingredients as vegetables and meats from over-cooking. Cream and cream-style soups will in all likelihood have "separated"; give them a whirl in the container of a food processor or blender and their smooth homogeneity will be restored; bring them to serving temperature over gentle heat. (See also Processor, page 5.)

Jellied soups (to serve): pour the completed soup into a shallow dish and allow it to cool to room temperature; chill it for at least 6 hours, or until it is thoroughly set; with a sharp knife, cut through the gelatin in a checkerboard pattern, making squares of about ½ inch. When the jellied soup is spooned into individual chilled dishes, the squares will separate into attractive sparkling cubes.

Milk: see Cream, page 3, and Scalding, page 5.

Pepper: please! fresh-ground, be it black or white. (Unless, of course, peppercorns are called for.)

Potato: an essential ingredient of many soups, potatoes tend to darken shortly after they are peeled and chopped or diced; to avoid this discoloration, cover the potato, whole or cut up, with cold water; when ready to use it, drain and add it to the recipe as directed. (See also Thickening Agents, page 6.)

Pots and pans (for soup-making): recipes yielding no more than 8 cupfuls—particularly cream and cream-style soups—may be successfully made in a 3-quart saucepan. A 5-quart enamelized-iron casserole is also ideal for such soups and for recipes making a somewhat larger quantity. All recipes may be made successfully in a soup kettle—any large pot holding up to 10 to 12 quarts. As a matter of fact, except for smaller-yield recipes of cream and cream-style soups (for which the large saucepan is ideal, as the confined space makes easier a smooth thickening of the soup), I prefer the soup kettle, a utensil sure to hold all the ingredients I care to combine in it and, at the same time, copious enough to permit of my skimming, stirring, and sampling.

Processor: I have two kitchen rules which apply to both processor and blender: 1) I never put more than 2 cupfuls of a mixture in the container because the appliance does a better job when the amount is smaller and because, in the case of a blender, there is less likelihood that the gadget will throw the mixture at the ceiling; 2) as for puréeing with a processor or blender any mixture that has been taken directly from the stove—don't! Allow the mixture to cool slightly; doing so will avoid eruptions within the appliance container which may be reminiscent of Old Faithful and which may also put you in danger of being scalded. When puréeing or making such sauces as *pesto genovese* and *rouille* with a processor, use the steel knife.

Puréeing: see Processor, above.

Refrigerating: all recipes in this book may be refrigerated. To heat refrigerated soup, allow it to come fully to room temperature and then, over gentle heat, bring it to your desired degree of hotness; this method will prevent scorching and/or overcooking of any solid ingredients. (See also Defatting Soups, page 3.)

Render: cooking bacon, salt pork, or other fatty meat until it is crisp and browned.

Scalding (milk and cream): scald milk and cream when making an acid soup—for example, Cream of Tomato; doing so is not necessary when making a bland one, such as Vichyssoise. If you make a habit of scalding milk and cream, you will indeed be surer of the resultant soup, and for this reason I recommend the additional step. (See Cream, page 3.) Scalding means to heat milk or cream just to the boiling point, but not above it. When a film shines or shimmers on the surface, the milk or cream has been heated enough to reduce its souring proclivities.

Serving soup: serve hot soups in heated cups or bowls and, if desired, from a heated tureen; the point of hot soup is to be just that—hot—and you will be surprised at how much longer it holds its heat if served in this way. By the same token, serve chilled and jellied soups in chilled dishes. Garnish the soup to make it visually attractive (my favorite garnish is fine-chopped parsley, which works successfully with any soup I can name). (See also Garnishes, page 231, and, in this section, Jellied Soups, page 4, and Refrigerating, page 5.)

Simmering: a slow cooking—simmering—of meats and vegetables is certainly the best way to assure a rich, full-bodied, flavorful stock or soup. Soups may cloud when they are simmered (cooked without boiling at about 200° F.) *if* they are contained by a tight-fitting lid; to avoid this pitfall, use a loose-fitting lid or leave a tight-fitting one slightly ajar.

Thickening agents:

BARLEY: 1 teaspoonful to 1 cupful of liquid, added at the start of cooking.

BEURRE MANIÉ: using a fork, blend until the mixture is smooth equal amounts of soft (not melted) butter and flour; add the *beurre manié* to the simmering broth or soup as directed, stirring constantly until the whole is thickened and smooth. A *beurre manié* of 4 tablespoonfuls of butter and 4 tablespoonfuls of flour will thicken 5 to 6 cupfuls of liquid, depending upon the density desired; suggested amounts of butter and flour are given in individual recipes. If a recipe calls for a particular spice, such as curry powder, add it to the *beurre manié* to assure a thorough blending.

CORNSTARCH: 1 teaspoonful to 1 cupful of liquid. See the directions for Flour, below.

EGG YOLK: 1 yolk to 1 cupful of liquid. Beat the yolks briefly, stir into them a little of the simmering liquid, then whisk into the bulk of the liquid the egg mixture; do not allow the soup to return to the boil.

FLOUR: 1½ teaspoonfuls to 1 tablespoonful (depending upon the degree of thickness desired) to 1 cupful of liquid. Make a paste of the flour and cold water; add the mixture to the simmering liquid, stirring for 5 minutes.

OATMEAL (quick-cooking): 1 teaspoonful to 1 cupful of liquid.

POTATO: ½ cupful of peeled, diced potato to 4 cupfuls of liquid. Cook the potato in the liquid for 25 minutes, or until it is very tender, and then purée the mixture.

RICE: 1 teaspoonful to 1 cupful of liquid. Cook the rice in the liquid for 20 minutes, or until it is very tender. Puréeing the mixture will make it somewhat thicker still.

ROUX: equal amounts of fat (usually butter) and flour cooked over gentle heat for a few minutes to rid the flour of any graininess or mealy taste. To the *roux* is added the liquid ingredient of the soup. To assure a smooth consistency, it is important to stir the mixture constantly until it is thickened. I find a *roux* of 3 tablespoonfuls of butter and 3 tablespoonfuls of flour adequate to thicken 4 cupfuls of liquid.

TAPIOCA (quick-cooking): ½ teaspoonful to 1 cupful of liquid. Cook the tapioca in the liquid, stirring frequently.

Wine: wine intensifies the saltiness of soup; when using it, guard against oversalting. Add it at the time of serving.

Madeira and sherry (not too dry) are recommended for Chicken and Veal Stock—¼ cupful to 4 cupfuls of stock.

Dry red wine enhances Beef Stock—½ cupful to 4 cupfuls of stock.

Dry white wine is a fine addition to Veal Stock and fish soups— ½ cupful to 4 cupfuls of stock or soup.

Do not allow soups to boil after the addition of wine.

Yield: you will notice that the yield of these recipes is always "about." The recipe will probably not be less than the amount suggested and it may well be more because the yield is based largely upon the *liquid* content of the completed soup; the solid ingredients add to the quantity. The yield also depends upon how much liquid was lost in cooking the soup, upon your measures of the ingredients (did you alter the suggested ones to your taste, as I hope you will?).

Statistical note: 4 cupfuls of soup will make 6 first-course servings or 4 main-course first helpings.

THICK SOUPS

Thick soups—a term which does not necessarily mean "thickened"—serve as a substantial first course or as the main dish of a meal. They may be made with Meat, Chicken, Fish, or Vegetable Stock, to which are added the various ingredients giving them their particular taste and consistency. The following recipes, I hope, will act as a point of departure for your own culinary adventures. I have found that thick soups taste better if made a day ahead of serving; during the time they "rest" the flavors meld.

Meat-stock Soups

BEEF SOUP
United States

Yield: about 14 cups
Preparation: about 4¼ hours

Attributed to Thomas Jefferson, who wrote in his daughter's cook-book a recipe yielding this soup.

---

3 tablespoons butter
1 beef soup bone with meat, sawed into 3-inch lengths (ask your butcher), the meat cut from the bone

In a skillet, heat the butter and in it brown the meat.

10 cups water

In a soup kettle, combine the beef bones, meat, and water. Bring the water to the boil, reduce the heat, and simmer the meat, covered, skimming as necessary, for 3 hours, or until the meat is very tender. (Add water to maintain the liquid volume.)

If desired, allow the broth to cool, refrigerate it overnight, and the following day remove the solidified fat.

2 large ribs celery, chopped, with their leaves
4 medium-size onions, peeled and chopped
2 parsnips, scraped and sliced thin

In the skillet, glaze the vegetables, using butter as necessary. To them, add about 2 cupfuls of the stock and cook them until tender. Add the vegetables to the contents of the kettle.

2 medium-size white turnips,
  scraped and chopped small
  Any other seasonal fresh
  vegetable, cut small
  Butter

1 small cabbage, cored and
  shredded
  Butter
  Salt
  Pepper

In the skillet, sauté the cabbage, stirring, until it is limp; use butter as necessary. Add the cabbage to the soup and simmer it for 15 minutes, or until it is tender. Season the soup to taste with salt and pepper.

VARIATION: *in Jefferson's day, this recipe would not have been considered a main-dish soup. You can make it so, however, by the addition of* Dumplings, *pages 235–36.*

BEEF AND APRICOT SOUP
Russia

Yield: about 12 cups
Preparation: about 3¾ hours

Serve the soup with pumpernickel or other black bread and sweet butter.

---

1 (2½-pound) piece chuck
  steak, the fat removed
  Water
1 bay leaf
2 teaspoons salt
6 peppercorns

In a soup kettle, arrange the meat, add water to cover by 1 inch; add the seasonings. Bring the water to the boil, reduce the heat, and simmer the meat, covered, skimming as necessary, for 2½ hours, or until it is tender.

Remove the meat; strain and reserve the broth. Cut the meat into bite-size pieces and reserve it. ▶

4 tablespoons butter
2 medium-size onions, peeled and chopped
4 large ripe tomatoes, peeled, seeded, and chopped
Reserved broth

In the soup kettle, heat the butter and in it cook the onion until golden. Add the tomato and cook the mixture, stirring occasionally, until any excess moisture has evaporated.

Add the reserved broth to the soup kettle.

1 cup dried apricots, quartered
5 medium-size potatoes, peeled and diced

To the contents of the kettle, add the apricot and potato. Return the broth to the boil, reduce the heat, and simmer the soup for 20 minutes, or until the potatoes are tender.

Reserved meat
Salt
Pepper
Fine-chopped parsley

Add the reserved meat, season the soup to taste with salt and pepper, and allow it to simmer for 10 minutes before serving it, garnished with parsley.

BEEF AND OKRA SOUP
United States

Yield: about 12 cups
Preparation: about 2¾ hours

A favorite in Alabama.

8 tablespoons butter
2 pounds lean beef, cut in small cubes

In a soup kettle, heat the butter and in it brown the beef.

1½ pounds okra, rinsed, trimmed, and cut in ½-inch rounds
2 large onions, peeled and sliced
12 large ripe tomatoes, peeled, seeded, and chopped
Boiling water

To the contents of the kettle, add the vegetables. Add boiling water to cover. Simmer the mixture, covered, for 1½ hours, skimming it as necessary.

Allow the soup to cool, refrigerate it overnight, and the following day remove any solidified fat.

4 cups boiling water
2 cups shelled fresh *or* frozen
  Lima beans
1 pound cured ham, diced
  Salt
  Pepper

Return the soup to the boil. Add the additional water, Lima beans, and ham. Simmer the soup for 30 minutes, or until the Lima beans are very tender. Season the soup to taste with salt and pepper.

BEEF AND VEGETABLE SOUP
United States

Yield: about 16 cups
Preparation: about 4½ hours

A rich, old-fashioned soup, enhanced by the addition of wine, "burgoo" was originally served at outdoor feasts in the South. Sometimes this dish is called "Kentucky burgoo."

---

1 (2-pound) beef *or* veal shin, sawed in pieces (ask your butcher)
10 cups water
1 tablespoon salt

In a soup kettle, combine these three ingredients. Bring the water to the boil, reduce the heat, and simmer the bones, covered, for 3 hours.

Remove and discard the bones, strain the broth. Allow it to cool, refrigerate it overnight, and the following day remove any solidified fat.

1 cup (packed) shredded cabbage
3 large carrots, scraped and sliced
2 large ribs celery, chopped
1 cup corn kernels
1 cup green peas
2 medium-size potatoes, peeled and diced
4 ripe tomatoes, peeled, seeded, and chopped *or* 1 (1-pound) can tomatoes, with their liquid

Bring the broth to the boil, add the vegetables, reduce the heat, and simmer them, covered, for 20 minutes, or until the potatoes are tender.

½ cup flour
½ cup dry red wine
1 tablespoon Worcestershire sauce
Salt
Pepper

In a skillet, brown the flour. Blend the flour with 1 cup of the broth until the mixture is smooth. Add it to the contents of the kettle, stirring until the soup is slightly thickened. Stir in the wine and Worcestershire sauce. Season the burgoo to taste with salt and pepper.

BEEF AND VEGETABLE SOUP
United States

Yield: about 12 cups
Preparation: about 3¾ hours

From Chicago, "Stockyard Beef Soup" is a wholesome one-dish meal.

2½ pounds beef shank, sawed into several pieces (ask your butcher), with its meat
3 tablespoons medium-size pearl barley
Tops from 3 large ribs celery, chopped
1 large clove garlic, peeled and chopped
2 medium-size onions, peeled and chopped
2 teaspoons salt
8 cups water

In a soup kettle, combine these seven ingredients. Bring the liquid to the boil, reduce the heat, and simmer the beef shank, covered, skimming as necessary, for 2¾ hours.

Remove the bones, cut any meat from them; dice and reserve it. Discard the bones.

Allow the broth to cool. Refrigerate the broth and the reserved meat overnight and the following day remove any solidified fat.

4 tablespoons butter
½ cup cut-up green beans (cut in 1-inch pieces)
½ cup fine-shredded cabbage
1 large carrot, scraped and sliced thin
3 large ribs celery, chopped
1 large potato, peeled and diced

In a skillet, heat the butter and in it cook these vegetables, stirring frequently, for 10 minutes. Transfer them to the soup kettle.

Return the broth to the boil, reduce the heat, and simmer the vegetables, covered, for 20 minutes, or until the potato is tender.

Reserved meat
1 cup fresh *or* frozen peas
1 cup fine-chopped fresh spinach *or* 1 (10-ounce) package frozen chopped spinach, fully thawed to room temperature and pressed dry in a colander
Salt
Pepper
Fine-chopped parsley

Add the meat, peas, and spinach; continue to simmer the soup for 10 minutes longer, or until the peas are tender. Season the soup to taste with salt and pepper. Serve it garnished with chopped parsley.

BEEF AND VEGETABLE SOUP WITH YOGURT
Afghanistan

Yield: about 10 cups
Preparation: about 2 hours

The secret of this one-dish meal lies in the addition of the yogurt and mint.

---

2 pounds ground chuck

Preheat the oven to 325° F. On top of the stove, in a flame-proof 5-quart casserole, brown the meat, breaking it up into small bits. Discard the excess fat.

1 large clove garlic, peeled and chopped fine
2 large onions, peeled and chopped
1 medium-size green pepper, seeded and chopped
1 (1-pound) can Italian tomatoes, with their liquid
½ teaspoon thyme
1 teaspoon sugar
1½ teaspoons salt
½ teaspoon pepper
2½ cups water

To the contents of the casserole, add the vegetables, seasonings, and water. Bake the mixture, covered, for 1 hour, stirring it occasionally.

1 (20-ounce) can red kidney beans
1 (20-ounce) can white kidney beans
2 cups plain yogurt
Chopped fresh mint *or* dried mint leaf flakes

To the casserole, add the kidney beans, undrained, and the yogurt. Stir the soup gently to blend it well. Return it to the oven for 15 minutes to heat thoroughly. When serving the soup, garnish it with mint.

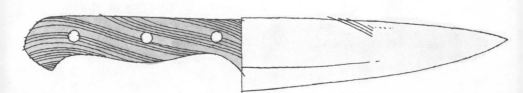

BEEF GUMBO
United States

Yield: about 14 cups
Preparation: about 4¼ hours

This Creole dish, a combination of French, Spanish, and African cooking in New Orleans, is named from the African Bantu word for "okra." The soup-stew is usually served over boiled rice and is sometimes made with seafood, salt pork, chicken and ham, in addition to beef. There are many recipes for gumbo; here is one and there are others on pages 39 and 55.

3 tablespoons butter *or* bacon fat
1 (3-pound) beef soup bone, with its meat

In a skillet, heat the butter and in it brown the meat on the bone.

10 cups water

Transfer the bone to a soup kettle, add the water, and bring it to the boil; reduce the heat and simmer the bone, covered, for 2 hours.

1 medium-size rib celery, with its leaves
6 sprigs parsley
1 medium-size onion, peeled and quartered
½ teaspoon paprika
1 teaspoon salt

To the contents of the kettle, add these five ingredients and continue to simmer the soup bone for an additional 30 minutes, or until the meat separates easily from the bone.

Remove the bone; cut the meat from it and reserve it. Discard the bone. Strain the stock, pressing to extract all liquid from the vegetables. Allow it to cool. Refrigerate the stock and the reserved meat overnight and the following day remove the solidified fat.

3 tablespoons butter
2 large ribs celery, chopped
¼ pound okra, rinsed, trimmed, and sliced in ½-inch rounds
2 medium-size onions, peeled and sliced thin

In the soup kettle, heat the butter and in it cook these vegetables until the onion is translucent. ▶

6 medium-size ripe tomatoes,
peeled, seeded, and
chopped
2½ tablespoons quick-cooking
tapioca
1 tablespoon sugar
Reserved stock

Reserved meat
Salt
Pepper
Fine-chopped parsley *or*
watercress

To the contents of the kettle, add these four ingredients. Return the stock to the boil, reduce the heat, and simmer the soup, covered, for 1 hour.

Add the reserved beef and heat it through. Season the soup to taste with salt and pepper. Serve the soup garnished with parsley or watercress.

GULYÁSLEVES
Hungarian Goulash Soup

Yield: about 10 cups
Preparation: about 2½ hours

Gulyásleves *is perhaps the most famous soup of a country where soups are an important part of the diet.*

3 tablespoons lard
3 medium-size onions, peeled
and chopped
1½ pounds beef chuck, cut in
1-inch cubes
2 tablespoons paprika
(preferably Hungarian
sweet)

In a soup kettle, melt the lard and in it cook the onion until translucent. Add the beef and paprika; brown the meat.

½ teaspoon caraway seed
  (optional)
1 large clove garlic, peeled
  and put through a press
  Zest of 1 small lemon
6 cups Beef Stock *or* 4
  (10½-ounce) cans beef
  broth plus water to equal 6
  cups

2 medium-size potatoes,
  peeled and diced
2 large ripe tomatoes, peeled,
  seeded, and chopped
  Salt
  Pepper

To the contents of the kettle, add these four ingredients. Bring the liquid to the boil, reduce the heat, and simmer the beef, covered, for 1½ hours, or until it is tender.

Allow the contents of the kettle to cool, refrigerate them overnight, and the following day remove any solidified fat.

Add the potato and tomato. Simmer the soup for 20 minutes, or until the potato is tender. Season the soup to taste with salt and pepper.

GROUND BEEF SOUP
Paraguay

Yield: about 10 cups
Preparation: about 50 minutes

It's the bananas that turn the trick.

6 cups water
1½ pounds lean ground beef

In a large saucepan, combine the water and ground beef. Bring the liquid to the boil, reduce the heat, and simmer the meat, covered, for 10 minutes. Break up any lumps that may form.

4 tablespoons butter
2 green bananas, peeled and
  cut in ½-inch rounds
2 large onions, peeled and
  chopped
2 large ripe tomatoes, peeled,
  seeded, and chopped
¼ cup raw natural rice
  Salt
  Pepper
  Fine-chopped parsley

In a skillet, heat the butter and in it sauté the banana, onion, and tomato, stirring, for 5 minutes, or until the onion is translucent. Add the mixture to the contents of the saucepan, together with the rice. Simmer the soup, covered, 30 minutes. Season the soup to taste with salt and pepper. Serve it garnished with chopped parsley.

KIDNEY SOUP
Netherlands

I found this dish warmly comforting one winter when in Holland to research Dutch cheese-making.

---

4 cups Beef or Chicken Stock *or* 3 (10½-ounce) cans beef or chicken broth
1 veal kidney, split, the fat removed, soaked for 1 hour in cold salted water, and rinsed.

In a large saucepan, combine the stock and kidney. Slowly bring the liquid to the boil, reduce the heat, and simmer the kidney, covered, for 15 minutes. Remove the kidney, dice and reserve it. Set aside the saucepan with stock.

3 tablespoons butter
6 large mushrooms, chopped
1 medium-size onion, peeled and chopped

In a skillet, heat the butter and in it, over gentle heat, sauté the mushrooms and onion until the onion is translucent.

3 tablespoons flour
Reserved stock

Into the onion mixture, stir the flour. Over gentle heat, cook it for a few minutes. Gradually add 1 cupful of the broth in which the kidney was cooked, stirring constantly until the mixture is thickened and smooth. Add it to the reserved stock in the large saucepan.

1 cup light cream, scalded
2 tablespoons Madeira wine
Reserved kidney
Salt
White pepper
Dill weed

Stir in the cream and Madeira. Add the kidney. Bring the soup to serving temperature and season it to taste with salt and pepper. Serve it garnished with a sprinkling of dill.

KIDNEY SOUP
Russia

Yield: about 10 cups
Preparation: about 45 minutes

Rassolnik *is as Russian as a balalaika.*

2 tablespoons medium-size pearl barley
4 medium-size carrots, scraped and cut in ¼-inch rounds
2 medium-size potatoes, peeled and cut in large dice
6 cups Beef Stock *or* 4 (10½-ounce) cans beef broth plus water to equal 6 cups

In a soup kettle, combine these four ingredients. Bring the liquid to the boil, reduce the heat, and simmer the mixture, covered, for 35 minutes, or until the barley is tender.

3 tablespoons butter
2 medium-size onions, peeled and chopped

In a skillet, heat the butter and in it cook the onion until translucent.

8 lamb kidneys, split lengthwise, the fat removed, and chopped coarse
1½ tablespoons flour

Add the kidney to the onion and cook the mixture, stirring, for 2 minutes. Stir in the flour and, over gentle heat, simmer the kidney, covered, for 10 minutes.

Into the contents of the skillet, stir 1 cupful of broth from the kettle. When the mixture is thickened and smooth, transfer it to the soup kettle.

3 small dill pickles, chopped fine
Salt
Pepper
Fine-chopped parsley
Sour cream

Add the pickle. Simmer the soup, covered, for 10 minutes. Season the soup to taste with salt and pepper. Serve it garnished with parsley. Offer the sour cream separately.

LAMB SOUP
India

Yield: about 9 cups
Preparation: about 2¼ hours

Sometimes called "white soup" (because of the addition of almond milk?) or "unknown soup" (because of its myriad flavors?).

---

5 cloves garlic, peeled
1 (1-inch) piece ginger root, chopped
⅓ cup water

In the container of a food processor or blender, combine these three ingredients and whirl them until the mixture is smooth. Reserve it.

2 pounds shoulder of lamb, cut in 1-inch cubes
1 large onion, peeled and chopped fine
Reserved garlic mixture
5 cups Beef Stock *or* 4 (10½-ounce) cans beef broth
2 bay leaves
¾ teaspoon powdered cumin
1 teaspoon sugar
1 teaspoon salt
½ teaspoon pepper

In a large saucepan or soup kettle, combine the lamb, onion, garlic mixture, and beef stock. Add the seasonings. Bring the liquid to the boil, reduce the heat, and simmer the lamb, covered, for 1½ hours, or until it is tender.

2 tablespoons blanched almonds
1 cup milk

While the lamb is cooking, soak the almonds in the milk for 30 minutes. In the container of a blender, whirl the almonds and milk until the mixture is smooth. Reserve it.

5 tablespoons whole-wheat flour

In a skillet, brown the flour, stirring it constantly. Transfer it to a mixing bowl and stir in 1 cupful of the broth. When the mixture is smooth, add it to the contents of the saucepan.

Reserved almond milk
Pinch of cayenne pepper (optional)
Chopped fresh mint leaves

Stir in the almond milk and cayenne pepper. Serve the soup garnished with mint.

LAMB SOUP
United States

Yield: about 10 cups
Preparation: about 2 hours

A soup from Pennsylvania Dutch country.

---

2 tablespoons butter
2 medium-size onions, peeled and chopped
1 pound shoulder of lamb, diced
1 bay leaf
1 teaspoon powdered cumin
2 tablespoons paprika
5 cups water *or* Lamb Stock *or* 3 cups water plus 2 (10½-ounce) cans beef broth

In a large saucepan, heat the butter and in it cook the onion until translucent. Add the lamb and brown it. Add the seasonings and liquid. Bring the liquid to the boil, reduce the heat, and simmer the lamb, covered, for 1¼ hours. Discard the bay leaf.

3 medium-size potatoes, peeled and diced

Add the potato and continue to simmer the mixture for 15 minutes, or until the lamb and potatoes are tender.

1 cup cut-up green beans (1-inch pieces)

Add the beans and simmer them for 10 minutes.

1 tablespoon flour
½ cup sour cream
Salt
Pepper

In a small mixing bowl, blend together the flour and sour cream. Add the mixture to the soup, stirring until it is thickened and smooth; do not allow it to boil. Season the soup to taste with salt and pepper.

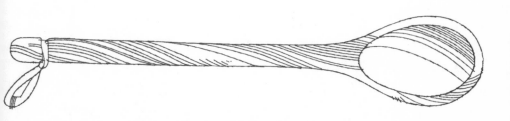

LAMB AND
BUTTERMILK SOUP
Wales

Yield: about 9 cups
Preparation: about 3 hours

How happily the flavors of lamb and buttermilk meld!

---

2 pounds lamb bones
1 pound lean lamb, in one
  piece if possible
2 large ribs celery, chopped,
  with their leaves
2 large leeks, rinsed and
  chopped, the white part only
2 small turnips, scraped and
  chopped
1 bay leaf
10 cups water

In a soup kettle, combine these seven ingredients. Bring the liquid to the boil, reduce the heat, and simmer the lamb, uncovered, for 2 hours.

Remove the bones and lamb; strain the broth and discard the residue. Dice the meat and return it, together with the bones, to the broth.

3 cups buttermilk

Over high heat, reduce the broth to 6 cupfuls. Stir in the buttermilk.

4 tablespoons soft butter
4 tablespoons flour

In a small mixing bowl, combine the butter and flour; using a fork, blend them until the mixture is smooth. Add the *beurre manié* to the simmering soup, stirring constantly until it is thickened and smooth.

Salt
Pepper
Fine-chopped parsley

Over very gentle heat, continue to simmer it, covered, for 10 minutes. Season the soup to taste with salt and pepper. Serve it garnished with chopped parsley.

SCOTCH BROTH
Scotland

Yield: about 12 cups
Preparation: about 3¼ hours

A satisfying one-dish meal from the Highlands.

---

1 pound lean, boneless stewing
lamb, cut in ½-inch cubes
1 pound lamb bones, tied in
cheesecloth
3 large carrots, scraped and cut
in ½-inch rounds
3 large ribs celery, chopped
coarse
3 large onions, peeled and
chopped coarse
4 small white turnips, scraped
and chopped coarse
Bouquet garni, page 2
2 teaspoons sugar
Water

In a soup kettle, combine these eight ingredients. The water should cover by 1 inch. Bring it to the boil and skim the surface as necessary. Reduce the heat and simmer the mixture, covered, for 1¾ hours.

½ cup medium-size pearl barley
Salt
Pepper

Add the barley and continue to simmer the soup, covered, for 35 minutes, or until the barley is tender. Season the soup to taste with salt and pepper.

Allow the soup to cool, refrigerate it overnight, and the following day remove any solidified fat.

½ cup chopped parsley

Reheat the soup. Just before serving stir in the parsley.

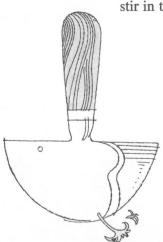

LAMB AND ZUCCHINI SOUP

Yield: about 10 cups
Preparation: about 1½ hours

An unusual lamb and lentil soup, enhanced by the addition of zucchini.

---

2 tablespoons butter
1 pound lean lamb, cut in 1-inch cubes

In a soup kettle, heat the butter and in it brown the lamb, a few cubes at a time.

2 large carrots, scraped and sliced
2 cloves garlic, peeled and chopped fine
3 leeks, rinsed and sliced thin, the white part only
2 white turnips, scraped and diced

To the contents of the kettle, add the vegetables. Cook them for 3 minutes, stirring constantly.

6 cups Lamb or Beef Stock *or* 4 (10½-ounce) cans beef broth plus water to equal 6 cups
1 cup lentils
1 bay leaf
1 teaspoon rosemary

Add the stock, lentils, and seasonings. Bring the liquid to the boil, reduce the heat, and simmer the lamb, covered, for 1 hour, or until it is tender.

Allow the mixture to cool, refrigerate it overnight, and the following day remove any solidified fat.

3 large zucchini, cut in ¼-inch rounds
2 tablespoons chopped fresh mint *or* 1 teaspoon dried mint
Salt
Pepper

Return the soup to the simmer, add the zucchini and mint; cook the zucchini for 10 minutes or until it is just tender. Season the soup to taste with salt and pepper.

MEATBALL SOUP

Yield: about 8 cups
Preparation: about 45 minutes

For the broth:

5 cups water plus 5 beef bouillon cubes *or* 4 (10½-ounce) cans beef broth

2 medium-size carrots, scraped and sliced thin

1½ cups fresh green peas *or* 1 (10-ounce) package frozen peas

6 scallions, trimmed and sliced thin

In a large saucepan, combine the bouillon water and vegetables. Bring the liquid to the boil, reduce the heat, and cook the vegetables, covered, for 5 minutes.

For the meatballs:

1½ pounds lean ground beef
¼ cup cracker crumbs
1 egg
¼ cup milk
¼ teaspoon basil
¼ teaspoon marjoram
¼ teaspoon rosemary
¼ teaspoon thyme
1 teaspoon salt
¼ teaspoon pepper

Meatballs
Salt
Pepper
Fine-chopped parsley

In a mixing bowl, combine the beef, cracker crumbs, egg, and milk. In a mortar, combine the herbs, salt, and pepper and, with a pestle, grind them to a powder. Add the mixture to the contents of the bowl. Knead the ingredients to blend them well. Roll the mixture into 36 small balls.

To the simmering contents of the saucepan, add the meatballs, a few at a time; the liquid should not stop simmering. Cook the meatballs, uncovered, for 5 minutes. Season the soup to taste with salt and pepper; serve it garnished with parsley.

MEATBALL SOUP
Bulgaria

Yield: about 10 cups
Preparation: about 35 minutes

For the broth:

8 cups Beef Stock *or* 6 (10½-ounce) cans beef broth

3 tablespoons raw natural rice

In a large saucepan, bring the stock to the boil, add the rice, reduce the heat, and simmer the rice, covered, for 15 minutes, or until it is tender. Strain and reserve it. Return the broth to the saucepan.

For the meatballs:

1 pound lean ground beef

2 eggs

1 small onion, peeled and chopped fine

1 tablespoon fine-chopped parsley

Reserved rice

1 teaspoon salt

¼ teaspoon pepper

In a mixing bowl, combine these seven ingredients and, stirring with a fork, blend them well.
Form the meat mixture into 36 small balls.

2 eggs

¼ cup plain yogurt

Fine-chopped parsley

Return the broth to a rolling boil, gently add the meatballs, reduce the heat, and simmer the soup, uncovered, for 10 minutes.

In a small mixing bowl, beat the eggs and yogurt to blend the mixture well. Away from the heat, just before serving, stir the mixture into the soup. Serve the soup garnished with chopped parsley.

MEATBALL AND NOODLE SOUP
Korea

Yield: about 10 cups
Preparation: about 1 hour

For the broth:

3 tablespoons vegetable oil

3 large cloves garlic, peeled and chopped fine

2 medium-size onions, peeled and chopped fine

4 scallions, trimmed and sliced thin

In a large saucepan, heat the oil and in it cook the garlic, onion, and scallions until translucent.

3 large ripe tomatoes, peeled, seeded, and chopped

Add the tomatoes and cook the mixture, uncovered, stirring frequently for 5 minutes.

¼ teaspoon red pepper flakes

1 tablespoon *tahini* (sesame seed purée)

3 tablespoons soy sauce

6 cups Beef Stock *or* 4 (10½-ounce) cans beef broth plus water to equal 6 cups

To the contents of the saucepan, add the seasonings and stock. Bring the liquid to the boil, reduce the heat, and simmer the mixture, covered, for 30 minutes. ▶

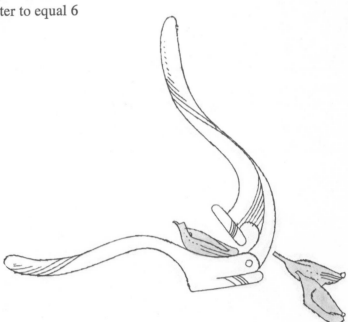

For the meatballs:
- 1 pound lean ground beef
- 1 medium-size onion, peeled and chopped fine
- ½ teaspoon ground ginger
- 1 teaspoon salt
- ¼ teaspoon pepper
- 1 egg, beaten

In a mixing bowl, combine all six ingredients. Using a fork, blend the mixture well. Form it into 36 small balls; reserve them.

½ cup vegetable oil

In a *wok,* heat the oil until it is very hot and in it cook the meatballs, a few at a time, until they are brown. With a slotted spoon, remove them to absorbent paper and reserve them.

¼ pound Chinese noodles
Salt
Reserved meatballs
Fine-chopped cilantro *or* parsley

Add the noodles to the broth and continue to simmer for 10 minutes, or until the noodles are tender. Season the broth to taste with salt. Stir in the meatballs. Serve the soup garnished with cilantro *or* parsley.

OXTAIL AND VEGETABLE SOUP
United States

Yield: about 12 cups
Preparation: about 4 hours

---

4 tablespoons bacon fat
3 pounds oxtail, disjointed
  Flour seasoned with salt and
  pepper

4 cups tomato juice
2 cups water
  Strained juice of 1
  medium-size lemon
2 bay leaves
2 teaspoons chili powder
1 teaspoon oregano
½ teaspoon rosemary
2 teaspoons sugar
1 tablespoon salt
½ teaspoon pepper
  Reserved oxtail

3 large carrots, scraped and
  sliced thin
3 medium-size onions, peeled
  and chopped
3 medium-size potatoes, peeled
  and diced
  Worcestershire sauce
  Salt
  Pepper

In a heavy flame-proof casserole, heat the bacon fat. Dredge the oxtail in the seasoned flour and brown it in the hot fat. Remove it to absorbent paper and reserve it.

To the fat remaining in the casserole, add the tomato juice and water. Over high heat, deglaze the casserole. Stir in the seasonings. Add the oxtail. Bring the liquid to the boil, reduce the heat, and simmer the oxtail, covered, for 2½ hours, or until the meat is very tender.

Allow the mixture to cool, refrigerate it overnight, and the following day remove any solidified fat.

Return the soup to the boil, add the carrot, onion, and potato and simmer them, covered, for 20 minutes, or until they are tender. Season the soup to taste with Worcestershire sauce, salt, and pepper. ►

VARIATIONS: *for a richer broth, add, in step two, 2 chicken backs and 1 pound of lean soup beef; for a greater variety of vegetables, add, in step four, either 2 cupfuls of chopped okra, 2 cupfuls of Lima beans, 1½ cupfuls of cut green beans, or 1 cupful of peas; add water as needed to cook the additional vegetables.*

For Oxtail and Black Bean Soup, add, in step two, for the last hour of cooking the oxtail, 1 cupful of black beans, which have been soaked overnight in water to cover, boiled for 5 minutes, and allowed to stand, covered, away from the heat for 1 hour. (Drain the beans before measuring them.)

POT AU FEU
France

Yield: about 14 cups
Preparation: about 3½ hours

Traditionally, the beef is served surrounded by the vegetables; the clear broth is offered separately.

---

2 pounds beef shank, in pieces
1 beef knuckle bone, tied in cheesecloth
10 cups water

In a flame-proof casserole, combine these three ingredients. Bring the liquid to the boil and skim the surface as necessary.

6 carrots, scraped and cut in 1-inch rounds
6 medium-size onions, peeled
3 medium-size white turnips, scraped and halved
Bouquet garni, page 2

Add the vegetables and *bouquet garni*. Return the liquid to the boil. Cover the casserole and transfer it to a preheated 350° oven for 3 hours. Discard the knuckle bone and *bouquet garni*.

Allow the casserole to cool, refrigerate it overnight, and the following day remove any solidified fat.

Salt
Pepper

Return the *pot au feu* to serving temperature and season it to taste with salt and pepper.

VARIATIONS: Petite Marmite *is the first cousin of pot au feu, with the addition of chicken parts and giblets. It is named for the utensil, originally earthenware, in which the recipe is cooked. For* Petite Marmite, *in step one omit the knuckle bone and add 1 pound of chicken gizzards and hearts plus serving-size pieces of chicken (your choice). Serve separately grated cheese and oven-dried slices of French bread.*

For Poule-au-pot, *use the giblets and 1 medium-size whole chicken.*

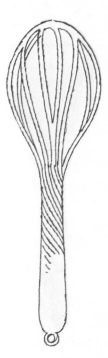

Tripe Soups. *I hold a special prejudice for tripe—for, not against, it. Properly cooked, it is tender, tasty, and very nourishing, being nearly 100 per cent protein.*

PHILADELPHIA PEPPER POT
United States

Yield: about 18 cups
Preparation: about 4¾ hours

During the winter of 1777–78, morale was low at Valley Forge. To bolster the spirits of his men, General Washington ordered a good meal to be served, but the cook had only tripe and scraps to work with. The result was this now-famous soup, called "Philadelphia" after the cook's hometown.

---

3 pounds honeycomb tripe
1 veal knuckle
1 large rib celery, chopped
1 large onion, peeled and chopped
1 medium-size green pepper, seeded and chopped
4 large ripe tomatoes, chopped
12 cups water
4 bay leaves
8 sprigs parsley

In a soup kettle, combine these nine ingredients. Bring the liquid to the boil, reduce the heat, and simmer the tripe and veal knuckle, covered, skimming as necessary, for 3 hours, or until the tripe is tender and the meat falls from the knuckle bone.

Strain the broth, forcing the vegetables through the sieve. Dice and return the tripe to the broth. Chop the meat and return it to the broth; discard the bone.

Allow the mixture to cool, refrigerate it overnight, and the following day remove any solidified fat.

4 medium-size potatoes, peeled
and diced
1 teaspoon marjoram
¾ teaspoon thyme
½ cup chopped parsley
Tabasco sauce
Salt

Dumplings, pages 235–36

Return the soup to the boil. Add the potatoes and herbs and simmer the mixture, covered, for 20 minutes, or until the potatoes are tender. Season the soup to taste with Tabasco sauce and salt.

Add dumpling dough and continue to simmer the pepper pot, without removing the cover, for 20 minutes.

TRIPE AND HOMINY SOUP
Mexico

Yield: about 14 cups
Preparation: about 4 hours

2 pounds honeycomb tripe, cut
in bite-size pieces
1 veal knuckle
2 carrots, scraped and cut in
½-inch rounds
2 ribs celery, chopped
4 cloves garlic, peeled and
halved lengthwise
2 onions, peeled, each stuck
with 2 whole cloves
6 sprigs parsley, tied with a
string
2 bay leaves
1 tablespoon chili powder
2 teaspoons cilantro
2 teaspoons sugar
2 teaspoons salt
Generous grating of pepper
Water

In a soup kettle, combine these fourteen ingredients. The water should cover by ½ inch. Bring the water to the boil, skimming as necessary; reduce the heat and simmer the meats, tightly covered, for 3 hours, or until the tripe is fork-tender. Discard the parsley and bay leaves.

Remove any meat from the veal knuckle, chop, and return it to the kettle; discard the skin and bones. Allow the kettle to cool, refrigerate it overnight, and the following day remove any solidified fat. ►

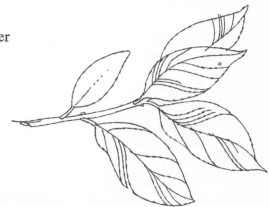

1 (6-ounce) can tomato paste
1 (29-ounce) can hominy
⅓ cup chopped parsley
1 bunch scallions, chopped, with as much green as is crisp
Zest of 1 medium-size lemon, cut in fine julienne
Salt
Pepper

Add the first five ingredients. Return the soup to the simmer and, over gentle heat, cook it, covered, for 30 minutes. Adjust the seasoning to taste with salt and pepper.

TRIPE AND ONION SOUP*

Yield: about 12 cups
Preparation: about 4¼ hours

2 pounds honeycomb tripe, cut in bite-size pieces
6 medium-size carrots, scraped and cut in ½-inch rounds
3 large ribs celery, chopped, with their leaves
1 bunch parsley, tied with a string
3 bay leaves
1 teaspoon sugar
2 teaspoons salt
Generous grating of pepper
Water

In a soup kettle with a tight-fitting lid, combine these nine ingredients. The water should cover by ½ inch. Bring the liquid to the boil, reduce the heat, and simmer the mixture, covered, for 3 hours, or until the tripe is fork-tender. Discard the parsley and bay leaves.

Allow the mixture to cool, refrigerate it overnight, and the following day remove any solidified fat.

18 small white onions, peeled	Reheat the broth. Add the onion and simmer the mixture, covered, for 15 minutes, or until the onion is tender.
6 tablespoons soft butter 6 tablespoons flour	In a small mixing bowl, combine the butter and flour. Using a fork, blend them until the mixture is smooth.
	To the contents of the kettle, add the *beurre manié,* stirring constantly until the mixture is thickened and smooth.
1 cup heavy cream, scalded Strained juice of 1 small lemon *or* lime Salt Fine-chopped parsley	Stir in the cream and the lemon or lime juice. Season the soup to taste with salt. Serve it garnished with parsely.

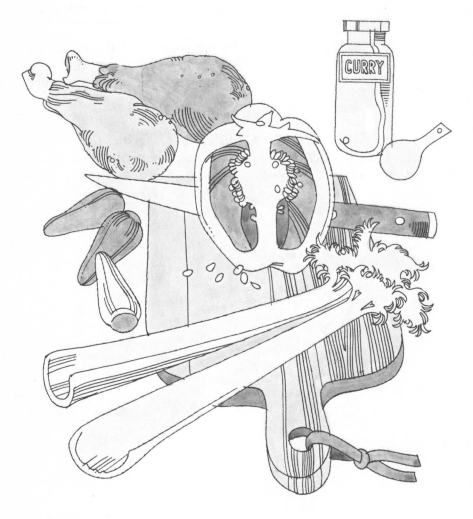

Poultry-stock Soups

CHICKEN GUMBO
United States

Yield: about 12 cups
Preparation: about 4 hours

Bones and trimmings from a roast chicken, duck, or turkey, the bones broken and the meat removed *or* 2 pounds chicken wing tips, necks, and backs
2 bay leaves
8 cups water

In a soup kettle, combine these three ingredients. Bring the liquid to the boil, reduce the heat, and simmer the bones or chicken parts, covered, for 1½ hours.

3 tablespoons bacon fat
3 ribs celery, chopped
1 green pepper, seeded and chopped
3 medium-size onions, peeled and chopped
3 tablespoons flour

In a skillet, heat the bacon fat and in it cook the vegetables for 5 minutes. Stir in the flour and, over gentle heat, cook the mixture for a few minutes. Reserve it.

Reserved vegetable mixture

Remove any meat from the bones, chop and return it to the broth. Discard the bones and skin. Stir in the vegetable mixture. Simmer the soup, covered, for 1 hour.

Allow the soup to cool, refrigerate it overnight, and the following day remove the solidified fat. ►

1¼	pounds okra, rinsed, trimmed, and cut in ½-inch rounds *or* 2 (10-ounce) packages frozen okra, cut in ½-inch rounds	Bring the soup to the simmer, add the okra, and continue to simmer it, covered, for 20 minutes. Season the soup to taste with salt and pepper.
	Salt	
	Pepper	
1	pint shucked oysters (optional)	Just before serving, stir in the oysters; simmer them for about 2 minutes or until their edges begin to curl.

CHICKEN RAGOUT SOUP
Austria

Yield: about 12 cups
Preparation: about 2½ hours

A favorite Austrian soup, running a close race with Gulyásleves *on pages 17–18, originally Hungarian, but which I discovered in Vienna.*

1½	pounds chicken thighs	In a soup kettle, combine these six ingredients. Bring the liquid to the boil, reduce the heat, and simmer the chicken and veal knuckle, skimming as necessary, for 1½ hours.
1	veal knuckle	
1	teaspoon sugar	
8	peppercorns	
2	teaspoons salt	
8	cups water	

Remove all meat from the bones; discard the skin and bones. Cut up the meat, and return it to the broth. Allow the broth to cool, refrigerate it overnight, and the following day remove the solidified fat.

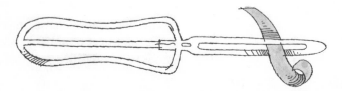

6 tablespoons butter	In a soup kettle, reheat the broth.
2 carrots, scraped and sliced thin	In a saucepan, heat the butter and in it cook the vegetables, stirring to coat them well, for 10 minutes.
2 large ribs celery, chopped, with their leaves	
2 medium-size onions, peeled and chopped	
2 parsnips, scraped and sliced thin	

2 tablespoons flour	Into the vegetables, stir the flour.
Salt	Add 2 cups of the broth, stirring
Pepper	until the mixture is thickened and
Dumplings, pages 235–36 (optional)	smooth. To the contents of the soup kettle, add the vegetable mixture.
Fine-chopped parsley	Simmer the soup, covered, for 30 minutes, or until the parsnips are tender. Season the soup to taste with salt and pepper. If desired, add dumpling dough and cook it as directed. Serve the soup garnished with chopped parsley.

COCKALEEKIE
Scotland

Yield: about 12 cups
Preparation: about 3¾ hours

This traditional soup is said to have been a favorite of Mary Queen of Scots'. Its name may derive from the custom that the losing bird in a cockfight was plucked, disjointed, tossed into a pot with several leeks for flavor, and stewed for the spectators to share following their sport. Cockaleekie requires long, slow cooking and, according to good Scotsmen, a very old bird, preferably a rooster.

1 four-pound stewing fowl, disjointed	In a soup kettle, combine these six ingredients. Bring the liquid to the
1 calf's foot or veal knuckle, split (optional)	boil, reduce the heat, and simmer the fowl (skimming as necessary if
Bouquet garni, page 2	you use the calf's foot), covered,
2 teaspoons sugar	for 2 hours. ▶
1 tablespoon salt	
8 cups water	

Allow the broth to cool. Discard the *bouquet garni*. Remove the meat from the bones; discard the skin and bones. Chop the meat and return it to the broth.

Refrigerate the broth overnight and the following day remove the solidified fat.

4 medium-size carrots, scraped and sliced
2 medium-size onions, peeled and chopped
½ cup medium-size pearl barley

To the broth, add the carrot, onion, and barley. Bring the broth to the boil, reduce the heat, and simmer the barley, covered, for 35 minutes, or until it is tender.

4 tablespoons butter
5 medium-size leeks, rinsed and chopped, with a little of the green part
Salt
Pepper
Fine-chopped parsley

In a skillet, heat the butter and in it cook the leeks until they are soft but not browned. Add them to the soup and continue to simmer it, covered, for 15 minutes. Season the soup to taste with salt and pepper. Serve it garnished with chopped parsley.

VARIATION: *if desired, a few dried pitted prunes and/or dried apricots may be added to the soup together with the leeks.*

MULLIGATAWNY

An Anglo-Indian soup, considerably changed from its native state by the colonists, mulligatawny derives its name from the Tamil molegu tune (the transliteration can be variously spelled in English), meaning "pepper water." The addition of rice to the soup dates from the time when the British in India served rice with virtually everything.

---

4 cloves garlic, peeled
1 (1½-inch) piece ginger root
3 tablespoons water

In the container of a food processor or blender, combine these three ingredients and whirl them until they are reduced to a smooth paste. Reserve it.

⅛ teaspoon cayenne (or more to taste)
½ teaspoon powdered cloves
½ teaspoon cilantro
½ teaspoon powdered cumin
1 tablespoon curry powder
½ teaspoon mace
¼ teaspoon pepper
  Reserved garlic-ginger paste

In a small mixing bowl, combine and sift together the dry spices. Add the reserved paste and blend the mixture well. Reserve it.

4 tablespoons chicken fat *or* butter
½ pound chicken giblets
½ pound shoulder of lamb, cut in large dice (optional)

In a soup kettle, heat the fat and in it brown the chicken giblets and lamb. With a slotted spoon, remove the meat and reserve it.

  Reserved spice mixture
3 medium-size carrots, scraped and cut in ¼-inch rounds
3 medium-size ribs celery, chopped
1 leek, rinsed and chopped, the white part only
2 large onions, peeled and chopped
1 medium-size green pepper, seeded and chopped
3 tablespoons flour

Discard all but 3 tablespoons of the fat. Into the remainder, stir the spice mixture. Add the vegetables and cook them, stirring, until the onion is translucent. Stir in the flour. ►

12 chicken thighs, the skin and fat removed

10 cups Chicken Stock *or* 7 (10½-ounce) cans chicken broth plus water to equal 10 cups
Reserved giblets and lamb

To the contents of the kettle, add the chicken thighs, stock, and giblets and lamb. Bring the liquid to the boil, reduce the heat, and simmer the mixture, covered, for 30 minutes.

⅔ cup raw natural rice

Add the rice and continue to simmer the soup, covered, for 15 minutes.

2 medium-size tart apples, peeled and diced
1 cup plain yogurt
2 tablespoons lemon juice (or more to taste)

Add the apple, yogurt, and lemon juice. Continue to simmer the soup for 15 minutes.

½ cup heavy cream, scalded
Salt
Toasted sliced almonds
Chopped parsley

Stir in the cream. Bring the soup to serving temperature. Season the soup to taste with salt. Serve it garnished with a sprinkling of almonds and parsley.

CHICKEN GIBLET AND BARLEY SOUP
Germany

Yield: about 10 cups
Preparation: about 2¼ hours

Easily made and with a very rich chicken flavor.

1½ pounds chicken giblets
2 pounds chicken wing tips, necks, and backs
3 medium-size ribs celery, chopped, with their leaves
2 cloves garlic, peeled and chopped
1 medium-size onion, stuck with 2 whole cloves
Bouquet garni, page 2
2 teaspoons sugar
2 teaspoons salt

In a soup kettle, combine these ten ingredients. Bring the liquid to the boil, reduce the heat, and simmer the mixture, covered, for 45 minutes, or until the giblets are tender.

6 peppercorns	
8 cups cold water	
⅔ cup medium-size pearl barley	Add the barley and continue to simmer the soup, covered, for 1 hour, or until the barley is very tender.
	Remove the chicken pieces except the giblets. Remove and cut up any usable meat from the chicken pieces and return it to kettle; discard the residue. Allow the soup to cool, refrigerate it overnight, and the following day remove the solidified fat.
½ cup fine-chopped parsley Salt Pepper	Bring the soup to serving temperature. Stir in the parsley. Season the soup to taste with salt and pepper.

CHICKEN AND HAM SOUP
England

Yield: about 8 cups
Preparation: about 50 minutes

This recipe is an adaptation of "Queen Victoria Soup," so called because of the monarch's fondness for it.

2 tablespoons butter	In a large saucepan, heat the butter
1 small onion, peeled and chopped	and in it cook the onion until it is golden.
3 medium-size ribs celery, chopped fine	To the contents of the saucepan, add the celery and mushrooms.
½ pound mushrooms, chopped fine	Over gentle heat, cook the mixture, stirring, for 10 minutes.
4 cups Chicken Stock *or* 3 (10½-ounce) cans chicken broth	Add these four ingredients and, over gentle heat, cook the mixture
½ cup diced cooked chicken	for 20 minutes, or until it is slightly
½ cup diced cooked ham	thickened. ▶
1 tablespoon quick-cooking tapioca	

2 cups light cream
Salt
White pepper
Fine-chopped parsley

Stir in the cream. Bring the soup to serving temperature and season it to taste with salt and pepper. Offer it garnished with parsley.

TURKEY SOUP*

Yield: about 14 cups
Preparation: about 2¾ hours

1 leftover turkey carcass, broken, plus any meat on it
2 cloves garlic, peeled and chopped
2 medium-size onions, peeled and chopped
2 bay leaves
1 teaspoon rubbed sage
1 tablespoon Worcestershire sauce
2 teaspoons sugar
1 tablespoon salt
8 cups water

In a soup kettle, combine these nine ingredients. Bring the water to the boil, reduce the heat, and simmer the turkey carcass, covered, for 1½ hours, or until the meat falls from the bones.

Remove the turkey carcass. Cut the meat from the bones, chop it up, and reserve it. Discard the carcass. Strain the broth. Allow the broth to cool. Refrigerate the broth and the reserved meat overnight, and the following day remove any solidified fat.

3 large carrots, scraped and cut into ½-inch rounds
3 large ribs celery, chopped
3 large ears corn, the kernels cut from them *or* 1 (10-ounce) package frozen corn kernels, fully thawed to room temperature
3 medium-size turnips, scraped and chopped
Reserved turkey meat

To the broth, add the vegetables. Bring the liquid to the boil, reduce the heat, and simmer the vegetables, covered, for 45 minutes, or until they are very tender. Stir in the turkey meat.

Salt
Pepper
Fine-chopped parsley *or*
Dumplings, pages 235–36

Season the soup to taste with salt and pepper. Serve it garnished with parsley or dumplings.

Fish Soups

FISH SOUP*

Yield: about 10 cups
Preparation: about 1½ hours

Bouillabaisse. *Or sort of, for the famous soup-stew from Marseilles can be made only right there, on the shores of the Mediterranean, where certain of the ingredients are native. Mentioned by Pliny and, to my best knowledge, every gastronome since, bouillabaisse has been the subject of heated arguments among cooks. No one seems to make it right—except in Marseilles, and even there opinions differ. Hence this version, my own.*

½ cup olive oil
4 medium-size onions, peeled and chopped

In a soup kettle, heat the oil and in it cook the onion until it is barely golden.

4 large cloves garlic, peeled and put through a press
1 (6-ounce) can tomato paste

Add the garlic and tomato paste; cook the mixture, stirring, for 5 minutes.

2 bay leaves
Zest of 1 medium-size orange
8 sprigs parsley, tied together
2 generous pinches of saffron
½ teaspoon thyme
2 teaspoons sugar
6 cups Fish Stock *or* 4 cups Fish Stock plus 1 (8-ounce) bottle clam juice and 1 cup dry white wine
Salt
Pepper

Into the contents of the kettle, stir the seasonings. Add the liquid; bring it to the boil, reduce the heat, and simmer the mixture, covered, for 30 minutes. Season the broth with salt and pepper to taste. ▶

3 pounds lean white-fleshed fish fillet, cut in bite-size pieces (cod, flounder, haddock, halibut, ocean perch, scrod, sole, turbot—use a variety)
Toasted rounds of French bread
Rouille, page 242 (optional)

Bring the broth to a rapid boil. Add the fish. Return the soup to the boil and cook the fish, uncovered, for 10 minutes, or until it flakes easily; do not overcook it. Serve the soup over rounds of hard-toasted French bread. Pass the *rouille* separately.

CODFISH SOUP
Spain

Yield: about 8 cups
Preparation: about 40 minutes

Codfish, fresh or dried, is important in Spanish cooking. This delicately seasoned soup is typical of the use of fresh cod.

3 tablespoons olive oil
2 cloves garlic, peeled and chopped fine
2 medium-size onions, peeled and chopped

In a large saucepan, heat the olive oil and in it cook the garlic and onion until translucent.

1 pound cod fillet, cut in bite-size pieces
2 cups clam juice
1 cup water
3 medium-size ripe tomatoes, peeled, seeded, and chopped *or* 1 (1-pound) can tomatoes, broken up
½ cup chopped parsley
Zests of 1 small lemon and 1 small orange, cut in fine julienne
½ teaspoon crumbled saffron
1 teaspoon salt
½ teaspoon pepper
Slices of toasted French bread (optional)

Add the codfish, stirring gently to coat it well with oil. To the contents of the saucepan, add these ingredients. Bring the liquid rapidly to the boil, reduce the heat, and simmer the soup, covered, for 15 minutes, or until the fish flakes easily. Serve the soup over a slice of toasted bread.

Chowders. *Our word "chowder" derives from the French* chaudière, *a large cauldron used in Brittany for making communal fish stews. In America, the classic chowder is based upon some pork product or other—salt pork, bacon—along with onion, potato, and milk.*

FISH CHOWDER
France

Yield: about 12 cups
Preparation: about 40 minutes

Aïgo sau, *sometimes spelled* aïgo saou, *is a fish stew from Provence and the Basque country.*

2½ pounds lean white-fleshed fish fillet, cut in bite-size pieces
6 medium potatoes, peeled and sliced thin
3 cloves garlic, peeled and chopped fine
1 large onion, peeled and sliced thin
2 large tomatoes, peeled, seeded, and chopped
Salt
Pepper
Bouquet garni of bay, celery and fennel leaves, orange peel, and parsley
⅓ cup olive oil
6 cups boiling water

In a large deep skillet or flame-proof casserole wiped with olive oil, arrange the fish in a single layer. Over it, layer the potatoes. Add the garlic and then the onion and tomato. Sprinkle with salt and pepper. Add the *bouquet garni.* Drizzle the olive oil over all. Add the water and cook the *aïgo sau,* covered, for 20 minutes, or until the potato is tender.

6 slices French bread, toasted and rubbed with garlic
Rouille, page 242

In each individual plate, arrange a slice of toast; over it, ladle the soup. Offer the *rouille* separately.

FISH CHOWDER*

Yield: about 12 cups
Preparation: about 40 minutes

This recipe is my adaptation of Cotriade, *a celebrated fish stew from Brittany.*

---

6 tablespoons butter
2 cloves garlic, peeled and chopped fine
6 medium-size onions, peeled and chopped

In a soup kettle, heat the butter and in it cook the garlic and onion until translucent.

6 medium-size potatoes,
  peeled and quartered
2 bay leaves
½ teaspoon marjoram
⅓ cup chopped parsley
½ teaspoon thyme
2 teaspoons salt
½ teaspoon pepper
8 cups water

2½ pounds lean white-fleshed
  fish fillet, cut in bite-size
  pieces
  Salt
  Pepper

To the contents of the kettle, add the potatoes, seasonings, and water. Bring the liquid to the boil, reduce the heat, and simmer the potatoes, covered, for 20 minutes, or until they are tender.

Add the fish fillet and continue to simmer the chowder, uncovered, for 10 minutes, or until the fish flakes easily. Season the chowder to taste with salt and pepper.

FISH CHOWDER
Hawaii

Yield: about 8 cups
Preparation: about 45 minutes

Not unlike our native fish chowder, at least in its basics, the Hawaiian version is given its special character by the use of fresh tuna as the principal ingredient and by the addition of ginger.

¼ pound salt pork, diced

In a large deep skillet or flame-proof casserole, render the salt pork; with a slotted spoon, remove it to absorbent paper and reserve.

3 medium-size onions, peeled
  and chopped

In the fat, cook the onion until translucent.

¾ teaspoon ground ginger
1½ pounds fresh tuna fish, cut
  in cubes

Stir in the ginger. Add the fish and, over low heat, cook it for 5 minutes, stirring.

3 medium-size potatoes,
  peeled and diced
3 cups boiling water
2 cups light cream, scalded
  Salt
  White pepper

Add the potato, pour over the water, and cook the mixture, covered, for 20 minutes, or until the potato is tender. Add the cream and season the chowder to taste with salt and pepper.

FISH CHOWDER
Mexico

Yield: about 10 cups
Preparation: about 45 minutes

½ cup olive oil
4 large onions, peeled and chopped

In a soup kettle, heat the oil and in it cook the onion until golden brown.

6 large ripe tomatoes, peeled, seeded, and chopped *or* 1 (28-ounce) can tomatoes, with their liquid
Bouquet garni, page 2
2 teaspoons chili powder
½ cup dry white wine

Add the tomatoes, *bouquet garni,* chili powder, and wine. Cook the mixture, uncovered, stirring often, until it is pasty. Discard the *bouquet garni.*

4 tablespoons flour
6 cups water
Salt
Pepper

Stir in the flour and continue to cook the mixture for a few minutes. Gradually add the water, stirring constantly until the mixture is thickened and smooth. Season it to taste with salt and pepper.

2½ pounds lean white-fleshed fish fillet, cut in bite-size pieces

Add the fish and simmer it, uncovered, for 10 minutes, or until it flakes easily.

FISH CHOWDER
United States

Yield: about 10 cups
Preparation: about 45 minutes

The classic New England recipe.

2½ pounds lean white-fleshed fish fillet, cut in bite-size pieces
2 cups water

In a saucepan, combine the fish fillet and water. Bring the liquid rapidly to the boil, reduce the heat, and simmer the fish, uncovered, for 10 minutes. Drain and reserve the fish; reserve the broth.

¼ pound salt pork, diced 2 large onions, peeled and chopped	In a soup kettle, render the salt pork until crisp. With a slotted spoon remove it to absorbent paper and reserve. Discard all but 4 tablespoons of the fat. In it, cook the onion until golden.
4 medium-size potatoes, peeled and diced Reserved fish broth	Into the contents of the soup kettle, stir the potato to coat it well. Add the reserved fish broth, bring it to the boil, reduce the heat, and simmer the potato for 20 minutes, or until it is tender.

Reserved fish
4 cups scalded milk *or* 2 cups
   milk and 2 cups cream,
   scalded together
½ teaspoon pepper
1 tablespoon salt
3 tablespoons soft butter
Reserved diced salt pork
	Add the reserved fish, milk, and seasonings. Float the butter on the surface of the chowder and, when it is melted, serve the soup garnished with the reserved diced salt pork.

SCALLOP CHOWDER
United States

Yield: about 10 cups
Preparation: about 45 minutes

A delicacy from Louisiana.

4 slices bacon, diced 2 medium-size onions, peeled and chopped	In a large saucepan, render the bacon. With a slotted spoon, remove it to absorbent paper and reserve it. In the fat, cook the onion until barely golden.
4 medium-size potatoes, peeled and diced 4 (8-ounce) bottles clam juice	Add the potato, stirring to coat it well. Add the clam juice, bring it to the boil, reduce the heat, and simmer the potato, covered, for 15 minutes.
4 ripe tomatoes, peeled, seeded, and chopped	Add the tomato and continue to simmer the mixture, covered, for 10 minutes. ▶

1 pound sea scallops, diced
4 soda crackers, ground to a
  powder in a mortar with pestle
1 cup light cream
  Worcestershire sauce
  Few drops of Tabasco
  sauce
  Salt
  Reserved diced bacon
  Fine-chopped parsley
  (optional)

Stir in the scallops, soda cracker powder, and cream. Bring the chowder just to the simmer for 4 minutes; do not allow it to boil. Season the chowder to taste with Worcestershire and Tabasco sauces and salt. Serve it garnished with the diced bacon and parsley.

SHRIMP CHOWDER
United States

Yield: about 8 cups
Preparation: about 1 hour

2½ cups water
 1 bay leaf
 1 rib celery, with its leaves

In a large saucepan, combine the water, bay leaf, and celery and boil, covered, for 5 minutes.

 2 pounds raw shrimp

Add the shrimp and cook them, uncovered, for 5 minutes, or until they turn pink. Strain the broth and reserve it. Shell and devein the shrimp; chop them coarse and reserve them.

¼ pound salt pork, diced

In a second large saucepan, render the salt pork until it is crisp and golden. With a slotted spoon, remove it to absorbent paper and reserve it. Discard all but 3 tablespoons of the fat.

 2 medium-size onions, peeled
   and chopped fine

In the fat, cook the onion until it is barely golden.

 3 medium-size potatoes,
   peeled and diced
   Reserved broth

Add the potato, stirring to coat it well. Add the broth. Bring the liquid to the boil, reduce the heat, and simmer the potato, covered, for 20 minutes, or until it is tender.

1½ cups milk
1 cup light cream
  Reserved shrimp
  Salt
  Pepper
  Reserved diced salt pork

Add the milk and cream. Stir in the shrimp. Bring the chowder to serving temperature. Season it to taste with salt and pepper. Serve it garnished with the diced salt pork.

VARIATION: *for* Shrimp Stew, *follow steps one and two as written; in step three, substitute 3 tablespoonfuls of butter for the salt pork; in step five, omit the potatoes entirely; in step six, increase the milk to 2 cupfuls and, in place of the light cream, use 2 cupfuls of heavy cream; use a little dry sherry when flavoring the stew; float 1 teaspoonful of soft butter on top of each serving and garnish it with chopped parsley.*

SHRIMP AND OYSTER GUMBO
United States

Yield: about 12 cups
Preparation: about 1 hour

A Louisiana recipe, made easily with two convenience foods.

---

1 pound raw shrimp

Peel and devein the shrimp. Reserve both shells and shrimp.

8 tablespoons butter
1 large onion, peeled and chopped
1 small sweet red pepper, seeded and chopped
6 tablespoons flour

In a flame-proof casserole, heat the butter and in it cook the onion and pepper until the onion is translucent. Stir in the flour and, over gentle heat, cook the mixture for a few minutes.

6 cups water

Gradually add the water, stirring constantly until the mixture is thickened and smooth.

  Reserved shrimp shells
1 (1-pound) can tomatoes, with their liquid
2 tablespoons gumbo filé powder

To the contents of the casserole, add the shells, tomato, and filé powder. Bring the mixture to the boil, reduce the heat, and simmer it, covered, for 30 minutes. Strain it and discard the residue. ▶

1 (10-ounce) package frozen okra, fully thawed to room temperature
1 pint shucked oysters, with their liquid
Reserved shrimp
Salt
Pepper
Cooked natural rice

Return the broth to the simmer. To it, add the okra, oysters, and shrimp. Simmer the gumbo, covered, for 5 minutes, or until the oysters curl at the edges and the shrimp turns pink. Season the dish to taste with salt and pepper. Serve it over cooked rice.

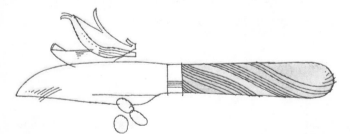

CIOPPINO
United States

Yield: about 12 cups
Preparation: about 2¼ hours

The famous fish soup-stew originated by Portuguese fishermen in California.

¼ cup olive oil
4 cloves garlic, peeled and chopped
1 medium-size onion, peeled and chopped
1 green pepper, seeded and chopped
4 scallions, chopped, with as much of the green as is crisp

In a soup kettle, heat the olive oil and in it cook the four vegetables for 5 minutes, or until the onion is translucent.

4 medium-size ripe tomatoes, peeled, seeded, and chopped
1 (8-ounce) can tomato purée
2 bay leaves
1 teaspoon salt
¼ teaspoon pepper

To the contents of the kettle, add these five ingredients. Simmer the mixture, covered, for 1 hour.

2 cups dry white wine
  Salt

Add the wine and continue simmering for 10 minutes. Adjust the seasoning.

12 littleneck clams in their shells, well scrubbed
1 large hard-shell crab, split, the legs disjointed
4 lobster tails, cracked
12 oysters in their shells, well scrubbed
½ pound raw shrimp, shelled and deveined

Return the broth to the boil, add the seafood, and cook the *cioppino*, covered, for 10 minutes, or until the clams and oysters have opened and the shrimp turns pink. Discard any clams and oysters that have not opened.

CLAM CHOWDER
United States

Yield: about 12 cups
Preparation: about 1½ hours

The Manhattan version.

---

2 dozen large hard-shell clams, well scrubbed *or* 3 (7-ounce) cans minced clams

Fresh clams: steam them open, strain and reserve the liquid, chop the clams coarse. Canned clams: strain and reserve the liquid. Reserve the clams.

Water

To the clam liquid add water to equal 4 cups. Reserve the liquid.

4 slices bacon, diced
½ cup chopped celery
1 large onion, peeled and chopped
1 small green pepper, seeded and chopped

In a soup kettle, render the bacon. Remove and reserve the diced bacon. In the fat, cook the celery, onion, and pepper, until the onion is golden brown.

2 large carrots, scraped and sliced thin
4 large potatoes, peeled and diced
2 medium-size white turnips, scraped and diced

Add the carrot, potato, and turnip, stirring to coat them well. ▸

Reserved clam liquid	Add the clam liquid, salt, and

Reserved clam liquid
1 teaspoon salt
¼ teaspoon pepper

Add the clam liquid, salt, and pepper. Bring the liquid to the boil, reduce the heat, and simmer the vegetables, covered, for 15 minutes, or until they are tender.

Reserved clams
3 cups canned tomatoes, with their liquid
¼ teaspoon thyme
Salt
Pepper
Reserved diced bacon
Fine-chopped parsley

Add the clams, tomato, and thyme. Simmer the chowder for 15 minutes longer. Season it to taste with salt and pepper. Serve the chowder garnished with the diced bacon and parsley.

CLAM CHOWDER
United States

Yield: about 12 cups
Preparation: about 1¼ hours

The New England version.

---

2 dozen large hard-shell clams, well scrubbed *or* 3 (7-ounce) cans minced clams

Fresh clams: steam them open, strain and reserve the liquid, chop the clams coarse. Canned clams: strain and reserve the liquid. Reserve the clams.

Water

To the clam liquid, add water to equal 4 cups. Reserve the liquid.

½ pound salt pork, diced
3 medium-size onions, peeled and chopped

In a soup kettle, render the salt pork. Remove and reserve the diced pork. Discard all but ⅓ cup of the fat. In the fat, cook the onion until golden.

4 large potatoes, peeled and diced
Reserved clam liquid
1 teaspoon salt
½ teaspoon white pepper

Add the potatoes, stirring to coat them well. Add the clam liquid, salt, and pepper. Bring the liquid to the boil, reduce the heat, and simmer the potatoes, covered, for 20 minutes, or until they are tender.

Reserved clams
2 cups milk
2 cups light cream
3 tablespoons butter
Reserved diced salt pork
Paprika *or* fine-chopped
parsley (optional)

Add the clams, milk, and cream. Bring the chowder to serving temperature but do not allow it to boil. Stir in the butter. Serve the chowder garnished with the diced salt pork and, if desired, a sprinkling of paprika or chopped parsley.

CRAB CHOWDER

Yield: about 8 cups
Preparation: about 40 minutes

Smooth, rich, and indecently good.

---

1 medium-size potato, peeled and diced
1 cup water

In a saucepan, combine the potato and water. Bring the water to the boil and cook the potato, covered, for 20 minutes, or until it is tender. Reserve the mixture.

2 teaspoons butter
1 small onion, peeled and grated

In a large saucepan, heat the butter and in it cook the onion for 3 minutes.

½ teaspoon paprika
1 teaspoon salt
¼ teaspoon white pepper
3 cups milk
1 cup light cream
2 tablespoons quick-cooking tapioca

Stir in the seasonings. Add the milk, cream, and tapioca. Bring the mixture rapidly to the boil, stirring constantly; reduce the heat and simmer it, uncovered, stirring, until the tapioca is dissolved and the liquid is smooth.

1½ cups flaked crab meat *or* 2 (6-ounce) cans crab meat
Reserved potato with its liquid
3 tablespoons cognac *or* dry sherry *or* Madeira
Fine-chopped parsley

Stir in the crab meat, potato, and potato liquid. Continue to simmer the soup for 10 minutes. At the time of serving, stir in the wine of your choice. Garnish the chowder with chopped parsley.

VARIATION: *for* Lobster Chowder, *follow the recipe as written, using an equal amount of cut-up lobster meat, with the tendons removed.*

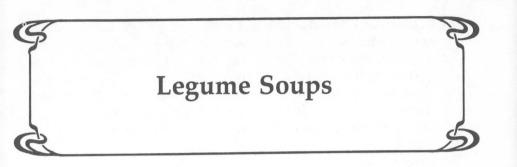

Legume Soups

Legumes, among man's earliest-cultivated food plants, have pods which open along two sides when the enclosed edible seeds are ripe. Beans, peas, chick-peas, soybeans, peanuts, and lentils are the best-known legumes, albeit over 10,000 species exist—among them clover and alfalfa, which are used as cattle fodder. Sometimes called "pulse," legumes, next to cereals, are our most important food plants, supplying a good portion of the nutritives we need for survival. Easily grown, legumes are generally dried, a fact which allows long and easy storage.

BAKED-BEAN SOUP
United States

Yield: about 9 cups
Preparation: 50 minutes

A traditional New England soup using leftover home-baked beans. The recipe may also be made with canned New England-style baked beans.

1½ cups leftover baked beans
1 large rib celery, chopped fine
1 medium-size onion, peeled and sliced thin
3 cups water

In a large saucepan, combine these four ingredients. Bring the liquid to the boil, reduce the heat, and simmer the beans, covered, for 30 minutes.

(If a thicker soup is desired, ½ or ¾ cupful of the beans, with their liquid, may be mashed or whirled in the container of a food processor or blender. Return the mashed beans or purée to the saucepan.) ▶

1½ cups strained stewed *or* canned tomatoes

3 cups Beef Stock *or* 2 (10½-ounce) cans beef bouillon plus water to equal 3 cups
Worcestershire sauce
Salt
Pepper
Thin-sliced hard-cooked egg
Lemon wedges

To the contents of the saucepan, add the tomatoes. Add the stock and bring the soup to serving temperature. Season it to taste with Worcestershire sauce, salt, and pepper. Serve the soup garnished with egg slices and lemon wedges.

BLACK BEAN SOUP
United States

Yield: about 10 cups
Preparation: about 4 hours

The addition of the ham bone gives a full, distinctive flavor; the soup is subtler, and equally good, when laced with sherry only. The soup may be served hot or chilled.

2 cups dried black beans
8 cups water

In a soup kettle, combine the beans and water. Bring the water to the boil and, over high heat, cook the beans for 10 minutes. Remove the kettle from the heat and allow it to stand, covered, for 1 hour.

1 ham bone (optional)
2 large ribs celery, chopped, with their leaves
1 medium-size onion, peeled and chopped
2 bay leaves

To the contents of the kettle, add these four ingredients. Return the water to the boil, reduce the heat, and simmer the beans, covered, for 3½ hours, or until they are very tender. (Add water as needed to maintain at least 6 cupfuls of liquid.) Discard the ham bone and bay leaves.

½ teaspoon dry mustard
2 teaspoons sugar
2 teaspoons salt
½ teaspoon pepper
Few drops of Tabasco sauce
Dry sherry

Add the seasonings and Tabasco sauce and sherry to taste. In the container of a food processor or blender, whirl the soup, about 2 cupfuls at a time, until it is smooth. Transfer it to a large saucepan.

Thin-sliced hard-cooked egg
Lemon wedges

Bring the soup to serving temperature, stirring. Serve it garnished with egg slices and lemon wedges.

VARIATION: *in place of the ham bone, use ½ pound of bacon, diced, rendered, and drained on absorbent paper. In some of the bacon fat, cook the celery and onion until the onion is translucent. Tie the bay leaves plus 1 teaspoonful of rosemary in cheesecloth; discard the herbs before processing the soup. Garnish the soup with the diced bacon, omitting the egg slices and lemon wedges.*

Or *omit the ham bone; to the completed soup, add ½ pound of shrimp, cooked, shelled, deveined, and chopped coarse.*

BLACK BEAN SOUP
Brazil

Yield: about 14 cups
Preparation: about 4 hours

Feijoda *is a popular dish, usually served with boiled rice—a full meal, indeed.*

---

2 cups dried black beans
10 cups water

In a soup kettle, combine the beans and water. Bring the water to the boil and, over high heat, cook the beans for 10 minutes. Remove the kettle from the heat and allow it to stand, covered, for 1 hour.

2 (4-ounce) packages dried beef, chopped

To the contents of the kettle, add the dried beef. Return the water to the boil, reduce the heat, and simmer the beans, covered, for 1 hour.

¼ pound slab bacon, cubed
1 unsalted pig's foot
½ pound smoked pork
½ pound Spanish garlic sausage, cut in rounds
½ pound smoked tongue

To the contents of the soup kettle, add these meats. Continue simmering the mixture, covered, for 2½ hours, or until the beans are very tender. Remove the pig's foot, smoked pork, and tongue. Dice the meat and return it to the kettle; discard any fat and bone. ►

2 tablespoons lard *or* butter
2 large cloves garlic, peeled and chopped
1 large onion, peeled and chopped
2 tablespoons chili powder

In a skillet, heat the lard and in it cook the garlic and onion until the onion is golden. Stir in the chili powder. Transfer the mixture to the soup kettle.

(If a thicker soup is desired, 1 or 2 cupfuls of the beans, with their liquid, may be mashed or whirled in the container of a food processor or blender. Return the mashed beans or purée to the kettle.)

Salt
Pepper
Boiled natural rice *or* lemon wedges (optional)

Bring the soup to serving temperature. Season the soup to taste with salt and pepper. Serve the soup over boiled rice or garnished with lemon wedges.

CHICK-PEA SOUP
Italy

Yield: about 8 cups
Preparation: about 2¼ hours

A Tuscan zuppa di ceci.

1 cup dried chick-peas
6 cups water
1 teaspoon rosemary, tied in cheesecloth
1 teaspoon salt

In a large saucepan, combine these four ingredients. Bring the liquid to the boil and cook the chick-peas, uncovered, for 5 minutes; remove the saucepan from the heat and allow it to stand, covered, for 1 hour.

Return the liquid to the boil, reduce the heat, and simmer the chick-peas, covered, for 1½ hours, or until they are very tender.

3 anchovy fillets	In the container of a food processor or blender, whirl the chick-peas with a little of their liquid, 2 cupfuls at a time, until they are reduced to a smooth purée. To one 2-cup batch of chick-peas, add the anchovy fillets before whirling the mixture. Return the purée to the saucepan, stirring to blend the mixture.
¼ cup olive oil 2 cloves garlic, peeled and put through a press 1 (6-ounce) can tomato paste	In a small saucepan, heat the olive oil and in it cook the garlic until it is brown. Add the flavored oil to the chick-pea mixture. Add the tomato paste, stirring until the mixture is well blended.
½ pound shell-shaped pasta Salt Pepper	Add the pasta and cook the soup, covered, for 10 minutes, or until the pasta is *al dente*. Season the soup to taste with salt and pepper.

VARIATIONS: *for* Chick-pea and Chorizo Soup (*Spain*), *in step two, add, for the final hour of cooking, 1½ cupfuls of fine-shredded cabbage and ¼ pound of* chorizo (or *pepperoni*), *sliced thin; do not purée the mixture; omit the anchovy fillets and use only 1 clove of garlic; omit the pasta.*

For Chick-pea and Lamb Soup (Harira *from Morocco*), *omit the anchovy and the pasta; add for the final hour of cooking the chick-peas, 1½ pounds diced lean lamb, 1 teaspoonful each of ginger, cinnamon, and turmeric, and a pinch of saffron; do not purée the mixture.*

CHICK-PEA AND VEGETABLE SOUP
Puerto Rico

Yield: about 14 cups
Preparation: about 4½ hours

2 unsalted pigs' feet 4 quarts water	In a soup kettle, combine the pigs' feet and water. Boil the pigs' feet, uncovered, for 1½ hours. ►

1 cup dried chick-peas,
   soaked overnight and
   drained
¼ pound cured ham, diced
2 tablespoons olive oil
1 medium-size onion, peeled
   and chopped
1 small green pepper, seeded
   and chopped
1 (6-ounce) can tomato paste
1½ teaspoons cilantro

To the contents of the soup kettle, add these seven ingredients. Simmer them, covered, for 1 hour.

½ pound cabbage, cored and
   shredded
3 medium-size potatoes,
   peeled and diced
½ pound pumpkin, pared and
   chopped
   Salt
   Pepper

Add these three vegetables and continue to simmer the soup, covered, for 45 minutes. Uncover the kettle for the last 30 minutes so that the soup will thicken somewhat. Season it to taste with salt and pepper.

DRIED
WHITE BEAN SOUP
France

Yield: about 12 cups
Preparation: about 1 hour

Fermière aux haricots blancs *is a popular provincial dish. Usually made with dried beans, I suggest using canned white kidney beans to shorten the preparation time.*

---

4 tablespoons butter
4 medium-size carrots, scraped
   and cut in ½-inch rounds
2 ribs celery, trimmed and
   chopped
1 large leek, thoroughly rinsed
   and chopped, the white part
   only
2 large onions, peeled and
   chopped
2 medium-size white turnips,
   scraped and chopped

In a soup kettle, heat the butter and in it cook the vegetables, stirring often, until the onion is translucent.

8 cups Chicken or Veal Stock, *or* 8 cups water and 8 chicken bouillon cubes
2 bay leaves
½ teaspoon thyme

To the vegetables, add the stock and herbs. Bring the liquid to the boil, reduce the heat, and simmer the vegetables, covered, for 30 minutes, or until the carrot and turnip are tender.

1 (20-ounce) can white kidney beans, with their liquid
Salt
Pepper
Toasted French bread
Chopped parsley

Stir in the beans. Season the soup to taste with salt and pepper. Continue to simmer it for 5 minutes. Serve the soup over the toasted bread, garnished with a generous sprinkling of chopped parsley.

DRIED BEAN SOUP
France

Yield: about 14 cups
Preparation: about 2¾ hours

A recipe from Provence. This soup is often called pistou, *in reality a French transliteration of the Italian name for the sauce traditionally accompanying it and which, indeed, came to Provence from Genoa.*

---

1 cup dried white beans
Water

In a soup kettle, combine the beans and water to cover by 1 inch. Bring the water to the boil and, over high heat, cook the beans, uncovered, for 5 minutes. Away from the heat, allow the beans to stand, covered, for 1 hour. Return the water to the boil, reduce the heat, and simmer the beans, covered, for 1½ hours, or until they are tender. Drain the beans, reserving them and the water.

4 tablespoons olive oil
3 cloves garlic, peeled and chopped
2 medium-size onions, peeled and sliced

In the soup kettle, heat the oil and in it cook the garlic and onion until golden. ▶

4 large ripe tomatoes, peeled,
seeded, and chopped

Add the tomatoes and cook the mixture, stirring, for 5 minutes.

½ pound green beans, trimmed
and cut in 1-inch pieces
2 large ribs celery, diced, with
their leaves
2 leeks, rinsed and chopped,
with some of their green
¼ cup chopped parsley
3 medium-size potatoes, peeled
and diced
2 medium-size zucchini, diced
Reserved beans
6 cups reserved bean water

To the contents of the soup kettle, add these seven ingredients. Bring the liquid to the boil, reduce the heat, and simmer the mixture, covered, for 20 minutes, or until the potato is tender.

¼ pound *vermicelli*
Salt
Pepper
Pesto Genovese, page 241

Stir in the *vermicelli* and continue to simmer the soup, covered, for 10 minutes or until the pasta is *al dente*. Season the soup to taste with salt and pepper.

Serve it garnished with *pesto genovese* or, if preferred, offer the sauce separately.

DRIED BEAN SOUP
Greece

Yield: about 10 cups
Preparation: about 2½ hours

Fassoulada *is a vegetarian dried-bean soup. Traditionally, the beans or black-eyed peas are left whole, but you may whirl 1 or 2 cupfuls of them, with their liquid, in the container of a food processor or blender; doing so yields a thicker soup.*

2 cups dried small white beans
or black-eyed peas
8 cups water

In a soup kettle, combine the beans and water. Bring the water to the boil and, over high heat, cook the beans, uncovered, for 5 minutes. Remove the kettle from the heat and allow it to stand, covered, for 1 hour.

½ cup olive oil	In a skillet, heat the olive oil and in
2 large carrots, scraped and sliced	it cook the vegetables, stirring, until the onion is golden brown.
1 large rib celery, chopped, with its leaves	
2 cloves garlic, peeled and chopped	
1 large onion, peeled and chopped	
1 (6-ounce) can tomato paste	Add the vegetables and olive oil to
2 bay leaves	the contents of the kettle. Add the
1 teaspoon mint	tomato paste, bay leaves, mint, and
¼ cup chopped parsley	parsley. Return the liquid to the
Salt	boil, reduce the heat, and simmer
Pepper	the soup, covered, for 2 hours. Season it to taste with salt and pepper.

DRIED BEAN SOUP
Japan

Yield: about 8 cups
Preparation: about 30 minutes

The soup may be made from dried beans; canned beans are suggested here to enable you to enjoy a delicate bean soup with a minimum of effort.

1 (20-ounce) can white kidney beans *or* chick-peas	In the container of a food processor or blender, whirl the beans and their liquid until the mixture is smooth.
2 tablespoons rice vinegar	To the purée, add the vinegar and
2 tablespoons *saki or* dry sherry	*saki;* whirl the mixture briefly to blend it well. Allow it to stand.
5 cups Beef Stock *or* 4 (10½-ounce) cans beef broth	In a large saucepan, combine the stock, carrot, and turnip. Bring the
2 medium-size carrots, scraped and grated	liquid to the boil, reduce the heat, and simmer the vegetables, covered,
2 medium-size white turnips, scraped and grated	for 10 minutes. ▶

Reserved bean purée	To the contents of the saucepan, add the bean purée, stirring to blend the mixture well. Simmer it, covered, for 5 minutes.
1 (7-ounce) can small Japanese shrimp, with their liquid 6 scallions, sliced thin, the white part only	Stir in the shrimp and scallions.
4 eggs 2 tablespoons soy sauce	In a small mixing bowl, beat together the egg and soy sauce. Add the mixture to the soup, stirring until the egg strands are set and soup is at serving temperature.

VARIATION: *in place of the shrimp, add 1 (7-ounce) can of minced clams, with their liquid; complete the recipe as directed.*

DRIED BEAN SOUP
Netherlands

Yield: about 10 cups
Preparation: about 2½ hours

A vegetarian soup.

2 cups dried white beans of your choice 8 cups water	In a soup kettle, combine the beans and water. Bring the water to the boil and, over high heat, cook the beans for 5 minutes. Remove the kettle from the heat and allow it to stand, covered, for 1 hour.
2 bay leaves 5 whole cloves 6 peppercorns	Tie the spices in cheesecloth and add them to the contents of the kettle. Return the water to the boil, reduce the heat, and simmer the beans, covered, for 1 hour, or until they are very tender. Discard the spices. In the container of a food processor or blender, whirl the beans with a little of their liquid, about 2 cupfuls at a time, until they are reduced to

a smooth purée. Return the purée to the kettle.

4 tablespoons lard *or* butter
2 large carrots, scraped and sliced
2 large ribs celery, chopped, with their leaves
2 medium-size leeks, rinsed and sliced, the white part only
2 medium-size onions, peeled and chopped

In a skillet, heat the lard and in it cook the vegetables, stirring, until the onion is translucent.

Worcestershire sauce
Salt
Pepper

Add the vegetable mixture to the contents of the kettle. Bring the soup to the simmer and continue cooking, covered, for 1 hour.
Season the soup to taste with Worcestershire sauce, salt, and pepper.

DRIED BEAN SOUP
United States

Yield: about 10 cups
Preparation: about 2½ hours

The recipe made famous by the United States Senate Restaurant.

---

2 cups dried Navy pea beans, rinsed
8 cups water

In a soup kettle, combine the beans and water. Bring the water to the boil and, over high heat, cook the beans, uncovered, for 5 minutes. Remove the kettle from the heat and allow it to stand, covered, for 1 hour.

1 large rib celery, diced
1 clove garlic, peeled and chopped fine
¾ pound smoked ham hock
1 large onion, peeled and chopped
2 medium-size potatoes, peeled, boiled, and mashed

To the contents of the soup kettle, add these five ingredients. Return the water to the boil, reduce the heat, and simmer the mixture, covered, for 2 hours, or until the beans are very tender.

Remove the ham hock. Cut the meat from it, chop, and return it to the soup; discard the fat and bone. ▶

Salt
Pepper

Bring the soup to serving temperature and season it to taste with salt and pepper.

VARIATIONS: *add, if desired, one or all of the following: 1 medium-size carrot, scraped and sliced thin, ½ green pepper, seeded and chopped, ½ cupful of tomato purée.*

DRIED BEAN AND VEGETABLE SOUP
France

Yield: about 16 cups
Preparation: about 3 hours

Garbure, *a word of Spanish origin, has about the same meaning as* "ragout." *The soup-stew which we know by this name is Basque with a tradition in Béarn of several centuries, where it is prepared in various ways according to the season.*

1 cup haricot *or* kidney *or* Navy beans
1 ham bone
8 cups water

In a soup kettle, combine the beans, ham bone, and water. Bring the liquid to the boil and cook the beans, uncovered, for 5 minutes. Remove the kettle from the heat and allow it to stand, covered, for 1 hour.

1 medium-size cabbage, cored and shredded
3 large carrots, scraped and cut in ½-inch rounds
3 cloves garlic, peeled and chopped fine
4 leeks, rinsed and chopped
2 medium-size onions, peeled and chopped
3 medium-size potatoes, peeled and chopped coarse
1 large turnip, peeled and chopped
¾ teaspoon thyme
2 teaspoons salt
½ teaspoon pepper

To the contents of the kettle, add these ten ingredients. Add water to cover, if necessary. Return the liquid to the boil, reduce the heat, and simmer the mixture, covered, for 45 minutes.

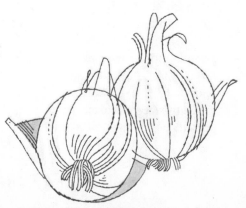

1 (1-pound) piece salt pork
8 chicken thighs, the skin
  removed (optional)

Add the salt pork and chicken; continue to simmer the soup, covered, for 45 minutes.

½ pound green beans, trimmed
  and cut in 1-inch pieces
1 sweet red pepper, seeded and
  chopped
  Salt
  Pepper
  Slices of toasted French
  bread

Add the beans and pepper; continue to simmer the soup, covered, for 25 minutes, or until the dried beans and green beans are tender. Adjust the seasoning to taste.

Serve the soup over the bread; slice the salt pork and offer it separately.

LENTIL SOUP

Yield: about 10 cups
Preparation: about 3 hours

Esau sold his birthright for a "mess of pottage," which was probably lentil soup made with the red lentils of Egypt. The brownish lentils from France are those more generally known in American supermarkets. Lentils are still a staple of Middle Eastern diet today, as they were in biblical times.

1 smoked ham butt
8 cups water
1 bay leaf

In a soup kettle, combine the ham butt, water, and bay leaf. Bring the liquid to the boil, reduce the heat, and simmer the ham butt, covered, for 1 hour. Discard the bay leaf.

2 carrots, scraped and sliced
2 ribs celery, chopped, with their
  leaves
1 large onion, peeled and
  chopped
2 cups lentils, rinsed
  Bouquet garni, page 2

To the contents of the kettle, add the vegetables, lentils, and *bouquet garni*. Simmer the soup, covered, for 1 hour, or until the lentils are tender. Discard the *bouquet garni*.

Remove the ham butt; cut the meat from it, dice, and reserve it; discard the bone.

In the container of a food processor or blender, whirl the soup, 2 cupfuls at a time, until it is smooth. Return it to a large saucepan. ►

Reserved diced ham	Stir in the diced ham. Bring the
Salt	soup to serving temperature. Season
Pepper	it to taste with salt and pepper.

VARIATIONS: *for* Middle Eastern Lentil Soup, *in step one in place of the ham butt, use 1 or 2 lamb shanks; in step two add 1 (6-ounce) can of tomato paste. Purée the soup only if you desire to do so and complete the recipe as written, garnishing each serving with fine-chopped fresh mint.*

For Cream of Lentil Soup, *in step one reduce the water to 6 cupfuls; complete the recipe as written, adding in step four 2 cupfuls of scalded light cream.*

GREEK LENTIL SOUP

Yield: about 10 cups
Preparation: about 3 hours

¼ cup olive oil
1 large clove garlic, peeled and chopped

In a soup kettle, heat the oil and cook the garlic until golden.

½ cup tomato sauce
8 cups Chicken Stock *or* 6 (10½-ounce) cans chicken broth
2 carrots, scraped and sliced
2 ribs celery, chopped, with their leaves
1 large onion, peeled and chopped
2 cups lentils, rinsed
Bouquet garni, page 2

Add the tomato sauce, chicken stock, carrots, celery, onion, lentils, and *bouquet garni.* Simmer the soup, covered, for 1 hour or until lentils are tender. Discard the *bouquet garni.*

(If desired, in the container of a food processor or blender, whirl the soup, 2 cupfuls at a time, until it is smooth. Return it to a large saucepan.)

Salt
Pepper
Red wine vinegar

Bring the soup to serving temperature. Season it to taste with salt and pepper. When serving the soup, add 1 teaspoonful of red wine vinegar to each dish.

LENTIL SOUP
Italy

Yield: about 10 cups
Preparation: about 2 hours

Zuppa alla paesana *is a Roman favorite.*

---

2 cups lentils
6 cups water

In a soup kettle, combine the lentils and water. Bring the liquid to the boil, reduce the heat, and simmer the lentils for 50 minutes, or until they are tender.

1 tablespoon butter
1 tablespoon olive oil
8 anchovy fillets, mashed to a paste
2 medium-size ribs celery, chopped, with their leaves
1 clove garlic, peeled and chopped
¼ cup fine-chopped parsley

In a skillet, heat the butter and oil and in it cook the anchovy, celery, garlic, and parsley, stirring, until the celery is soft.

4 large ripe tomatoes, peeled, seeded, and chopped

Add the tomato to the contents of the skillet and simmer the mixture for 25 minutes. Then, to the contents of the kettle, add the celery-tomato mixture and simmer the soup for 10 minutes longer.

½ cup shell-shaped pasta
Salt
Pepper
Grated Parmesan cheese

Add the pasta and cook it until it is just *al dente*. Season the soup to taste with salt and pepper. Offer the grated cheese separately.

PEANUT SOUP
United States

Yield: about 6 cups
Preparation: about 40 minutes

A rich soup from the tidewater region of Virginia and North Carolina.

---

2 tablespoons butter
1 medium-size rib celery, chopped fine
6 scallions, trimmed and sliced thin, with as much of the green as is crisp
3 tablespoons flour

In a large saucepan, heat the butter and in it cook the celery and scallions until translucent. Stir in the flour and, over gentle heat, cook the mixture for a few minutes.

2 cups Chicken Stock *or* 1 (10½-ounce) can chicken broth plus water to equal 2 cups
2 cups milk

Gradually add the stock and milk, stirring constantly, until the mixture is thickened and smooth.

Strain the mixture and, in the container of a food processor or blender, reduce the vegetables to a smooth purée. Return the purée to the liquid.

½ cup smooth peanut butter
Strained juice of ½ medium-size lemon
Few drops of Tabasco sauce
Salt

To the liquid, add the peanut butter. Using a rotary beater, blend the mixture until it is smooth. Season the soup to taste with the lemon juice, Tabasco sauce, and salt.

Chopped chives
Crushed peanuts

Bring the soup to serving temperature; do not allow it to boil. Offer it garnished with chives and peanuts.

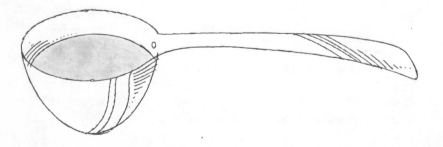

DRIED RED PEA SOUP
Jamaica

Yield: about 10 cups
Preparation: about 4½ hours

A recipe I enjoyed while visiting friends in Jamaica.

---

2 cups dried red peas, rinsed
8 cups water
½ teaspoon marjoram
½ teaspoon thyme
2 teaspoons salt
½ teaspoon pepper

¼ pound salt pork, diced
1 rib celery, chopped, with its leaves
1 medium-size onion, peeled and chopped
¼ cup chopped parsley

1 bunch scallions, trimmed and chopped, with as much of the green as is crisp
2 large ripe tomatoes, peeled, seeded, and chopped
Salt
Pepper
Fine-chopped parsley

In a soup kettle, combine the red peas and water. Add the seasonings. Bring the liquid to the boil, reduce the heat, and simmer the red peas, covered, for 2½ hours.

Add the salt pork and vegetables. Continue to simmer the mixture, covered, for 1½ hours, or until the red peas are very tender.

(If desired, you may allow the mixture to cool and then, in the container of a food processor or blender, whirl it, 2 cupfuls at a time, until it is smooth.)

To the hot soup, add the scallions and tomatoes. Continue to simmer the soup for 15 minutes, stirring often.

Season the soup to taste with salt and pepper. Serve it garnished with parsley.

VARIATIONS: *all Jamaican legume soups may be made from this basic recipe; you need only vary the principal ingredient: cow peas, black-eyed peas, butter beans, and so forth.*

SPLIT PEA SOUP
India

Yield: about 10 cups
Preparation: about 2 hours

Exotic and spicy—very good!

---

2 cups green split peas
8 cups Chicken Stock *or* 6
   (10½-ounce) cans chicken
   broth

In a soup kettle, combine the split peas and stock. Bring the liquid to the boil and, over high heat, cook the peas, uncovered, for 5 minutes. Away from the heat, allow them to stand, covered, for 1 hour.

15 whole cloves
¾ teaspoon cumin seed
24 peppercorns
2 teaspoons sugar
1 teaspoon turmeric
   Salt

Tie the spices in a double thickness of cheesecloth. Add the bag to the contents of the soup kettle. Stir in the sugar and turmeric.

Return the liquid to the boil, reduce the heat, and simmer the split peas, covered, for 1½ hours, or until they are tender. Squeeze the cheesecloth over the kettle and discard it. Season the soup to taste with salt.

(If desired, the soup may be whirled, 2 cupfuls at a time, in the container of a food processor or blender until it is smooth.)

SPLIT PEA SOUP
Netherlands

Yield: about 14 cups
Preparation: about 4¼ hours

Holland's Erwtensoep *is given a characteristic smoky taste by the bacon and* wurst.

---

2 cups green split peas
1 unsalted pig's foot
2 bay leaves

Preheat the oven to 300°. In a 6-quart oven-proof casserole, combine the split peas, pig's foot, and

1½ teaspoons salt
6 peppercorns
1 teaspoon sugar
6 cups boiling water

¼ pound bacon, diced

3 tablespoons reserved fat
3 medium-size ribs celery, chopped, with some of the leaves
2 large leeks, rinsed and sliced, the white part only
2 medium-size onions, peeled and chopped
Reserved diced bacon
½ cup chopped parsley

8 smoked *wurst or* frankfurters, cut in ¼-inch rounds
Remaining bacon fat
Reserved pig's foot meat

Croutons, page 234 (optional)

seasonings; over them, pour the boiling water. Place the casserole, covered, in the preheated oven for 2 hours.

In a skillet, render the bacon crisp; drain it on absorbent paper and reserve it. Reserve the fat.

In the fat, cook the three vegetables until the onion is translucent. When the casserole has cooked for 2 hours, add the vegetable mixture and the bacon and parsley to the contents of the casserole.
Stir the soup well.

Continue to bake the casserole for 1½ hours, or until the pig's foot is very tender. Remove it from the casserole; discard the skin and bones; chop the meat coarse and reserve it.

Brown the *wurst* in the bacon fat; drain the *wurst* on absorbent paper. Into the contents of the casserole, stir the pig's foot meat and the prepared *wurst*.

Serve the soup garnished with croutons.

VARIATION: *for Danish-style* Split Pea Soup, *add to the vegetables when cooking them in the bacon fat 3 medium-size carrots, scraped and cut in ⅛-inch rounds.*

SPLIT PEA SOUP
United States

Yield: about 12 cups
Preparation: about 3½ hours

The Yankee classic.

---

2 cups green split peas
1 medium-size carrot, scraped and chopped
1 large rib celery, chopped
1 ham bone
1 large onion, peeled and chopped
¼ cup chopped parsley leaves
2 bay leaves
  Pinch of rosemary
  Pinch of thyme
10 cups water

  Milk *or* water
  Worcestershire sauce
  Salt
  Pepper
  Croutons, page 234
  (optional)

In a soup kettle, combine these ingredients. Bring the liquid to the boil, reduce the heat, and simmer the mixture, covered, stirring occasionally, for 1½ hours, or until the peas are very tender. Discard the ham bone and bay leaves.

In the container of a food processor or blender, whirl the mixture, 2 cupfuls at a time, until it is smooth. Transfer the purée to a large saucepan.

Add milk to obtain the desired consistency. Bring the soup to serving temperature. Season the soup to taste with Worcestershire sauce, salt, and pepper. Serve it garnished with croutons.

VARIATIONS: *for* Beef Split Pea Soup, *in step one omit the ham bone and, in place of the water, use 10 cupfuls of Beef Stock or 8 (10½-ounce) cans of beef broth; add 1 (8-ounce) can of tomato purée; in step three, in place of the Worcestershire sauce, use ¼ cupful dry sherry. If desired, in step three add 2 cupfuls of diced cooked beef.*

The basic recipe for Split Pea Soup *may be used to make soup from an equal quantity of dried white beans, chick-peas, fava beans, yellow split peas, red peas, or Lima beans. The cooking time will vary depending upon your choice of legume.*

YELLOW SPLIT PEA SOUP
Sweden

Yield: about 10 cups
Preparation: about 2 hours

2 medium onions, peeled and sliced
1½ cups yellow split peas
1 (1-pound) piece salt pork
¾ teaspoon ground ginger
1 teaspoon marjoram
8 cups water

In a soup kettle, combine these six ingredients. Bring the liquid to the boil, reduce the heat, and simmer the mixture, covered, for 1½ hours, or until the peas and pork are tender.

Remove the pork, slice, and reserve it.

(If desired, you may whirl the split peas and broth, 2 cupfuls at a time, in the container of a food processor or blender until it is smooth. Transfer it to a large saucepan.)

Salt
Pepper
Dill weed
Reserved salt pork slices, heated
Mustard

Bring the soup to serving temperature. Season the soup to taste with salt and pepper. Serve it garnished with dill. Offer the salt pork slices separately with mustard.

Vegetable Soups

Vegetable soups are by far the most numerous of the "thick soup" category. They may be made with Beef, Chicken, Veal, or Vegetable Stock—or, for a "thinner" soup, with water flavored with bouillon cubes or powder—but the succulent, tender vegetables swimming in their broth are the stars of the performance, lending their special flavors to the delicious bouquet of these homely soups.

FRESH VEGETABLE SOUP

Yield: about 10 cups
Preparation: about 40 minutes

6 cups Chicken Stock *or* 4 (10½-ounce) cans chicken broth plus water to equal 6 cups
1 clove garlic, peeled and put through a press
½ teaspoon basil
½ teaspoon celery seed
¼ teaspoon ground ginger
¾ teaspoon savory
½ teaspoon thyme
1 tablespoon salt
½ teaspoon pepper

In a large saucepan or soup kettle, combine these nine ingredients. Bring the stock to the boil, reduce the heat, and simmer the seasonings, covered, for 10 minutes.

2 large carrots, scraped and shredded
3 large onions, peeled and sliced thin

Prepare the vegetables and add them to the broth; return the liquid to the boil and cook them, covered, for 15 minutes, or until they are ▶

1 medium-size potato, peeled
   and grated
3 large ripe tomatoes, peeled,
   seeded, and chopped
1 medium-size white turnip,
   scraped and grated
   Sugar
   Salt
   Pepper
   Pesto genvoese, page 241 *or*
   sour cream (both optional)

just tender. Season the soup to taste
with sugar, salt, and pepper. Serve
the soup garnished with either *pesto
genovese* or sour cream.

VEGETABLE SOUP

Yield: about 12 cups
Preparation: about 3½ hours

3 pounds beef shank, sawed in
   several pieces (ask your
   butcher)
2 bay leaves
¾ teaspoon marjoram
¾ teaspoon oregano
6 peppercorns
2 teaspoons sugar
1 tablespoon salt
8 cups water

In a soup kettle, combine these
eight ingredients. Bring the liquid
to the boil, reduce the heat, and
simmer the beef shank for 2 hours.
Strain the broth and reserve it. Remove any meat from the bones,
chop, and reserve it. Discard the
bones.
Allow the broth to cool. Refrigerate
the broth and the reserved meat
overnight, and the following day remove any solidified fat.

3 medium-size carrots, scraped
   and cut in ½-inch rounds
3 large ribs celery, chopped
1 (20-ounce) can red kidney
   beans, with their liquid
3 medium-size onions, peeled
   and quartered
4 large ripe tomatoes, peeled,
   seeded, and chopped *or* 1
   (1-pound) can tomatoes,
   with their liquid
1 medium-size turnip, scraped
   and diced

To the broth, add the vegetables.
Bring the liquid to the boil, reduce
the heat, and simmer them, covered, for 1 hour, or until they are
very tender. Stir in the reserved
meat. Season the soup to taste, if
necessary, with salt and pepper.
Serve it garnished with parsley.

Reserved meat
Salt
Pepper
Fine-chopped parsley

VARIATIONS: *for* Vegetable Soup with Barley (*Poland*), *in step three omit the kidney beans and use in their place ⅔ cup medium-size pearl barley.*

For Vegetable Soup with Garlic (*Majorca*), *in step three add 4 large cloves garlic, peeled and chopped.*

For Vegetable and Sausage Soup (*Poland*), *in step three add 1 pound* kielbasa, *sliced thin.*

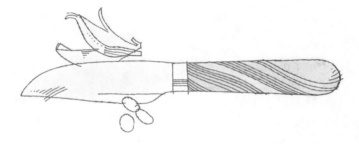

VEGETABLE SOUP
France

Yield: about 12 cups
Preparation: about 1 hour

A one-dish meal from the Auvergne.

---

6 slices bacon, diced	In a flame-proof casserole, render the bacon until crisp. With a slotted spoon, remove it to absorbent paper and reserve.
3 medium-size carrots, scraped and sliced thin 1 large clove garlic, peeled and chopped 1 medium-size onion, peeled and chopped 3 medium-size white turnips, scraped and diced	In the remaining fat, cook these four vegetables until the onion is translucent. ▶

1 small cabbage, cut into eighths and cored
6 cups water

Add the cabbage, spoon the other vegetables over it, and continue to cook the mixture for 5 minutes. Add the water, bring it to the boil, reduce the heat to medium, and cook the vegetables, covered, for 25 minutes.

6 small new potatoes, peeled and cut in ½-inch slices
Salt
Pepper
Reserved diced bacon
Fine-chopped parsley
Slices of toasted dry bread

Add the potato and continue to cook the soup for 20 minutes, or until the potato is tender. Season the soup to taste with salt and pepper. Serve it, garnished with the diced bacon and parsley, over the toast.

VEGETABLE SOUP
United States

Yield: about 10 cups
Preparation: about 2¾ hours

Known as "Black Kettle," this soup is native to Kentucky.

1 (2-pound) veal shin, the bone sawed into three pieces and cracked (ask your butcher)
8 cups water
Bouquet garni, page 2

In a soup kettle, combine these three ingredients. Bring the water to the boil, reduce the heat, and simmer the veal bones, covered, skimming as necessary, for 1 hour. Discard the *bouquet garni.*

Kernels cut from 3 ears of corn
¼ pound okra, rinsed, trimmed and cut in ½-inch pieces
2 medium-size potatoes, peeled and chopped coarse
2 large ripe tomatoes

To the contents of the kettle, add these four vegetables. Continue simmering the mixture for 1 hour.

Strain the broth and reserve it. Discard the veal bones. In the container of a food processor or blender, purée the vegetables; return the purée to the broth.

3 tablespoons flour 3 tablespoons soft butter	In a skillet, brown the flour. In a small mixing bowl, combine the browned flour and butter and blend the mixture until it is smooth. Add the *beurre manié* to the soup and stir constantly until the broth is somewhat thickened.
4 tablespoons currant jelly 1½ tablespoons Worcestershire sauce Salt Pepper	Stir in the currant jelly and Worcestershire sauce. Season the soup to taste with salt and pepper.

BORSCH
Russia and Poland

Yield: about 10 cups
Preparation: about 30 minutes

There are more recipes than spellings for this the most celebrated of Slav soups. There are thick borschs and thin borschs, hot borschs and cold borschs. Not all borschs are made with beets, albeit many are. Natively, nearly all have a basis of kvas, *a fermented liquid, used also as a drink, made from barley or rye, yeast, sugar, raisins, water, and sometimes mint.*

6 cups Beef Stock *or* 4 (10½-ounce) cans beef broth plus water to equal 6 cups 6 medium-size beets, scraped and grated 1 medium-size onion, peeled and chopped fine 1½ cups shredded cabbage	In a soup kettle, combine these four ingredients. Bring the liquid to the boil, reduce the heat, and simmer the vegetables, covered, for 25 minutes, or until they are tender.
1 tablespoon red wine vinegar Salt Pepper Sour Cream	Stir in the vinegar. Season the soup to taste with salt and pepper. Serve it garnished with sour cream.

Cabbage Soups. *The robust, distinctive flavor of cabbage does does not necessarily require real stock or broth to enhance it; in these recipes, water flavored with bouillon cubes is sometimes suggested as the cooking liquid, thus enabling you to save precious homemade stock or to economize by omitting canned broth.*

CABBAGE SOUP

Yield: about 9 cups
Preparation: about 1 hour

4 tablespoons butter
2 medium-size carrots, scraped
2 medium-size onions, peeled and chopped fine
1 parsnip, scraped and grated
1 small head cabbage, cored and shredded
6 cups water
6 bouillon cubes
2 bay leaves
1 teaspoon powdered cumin
2 teaspoons sugar
  Salt
  White pepper
  Sour cream

In a soup kettle, heat the butter and in it, over gentle heat, cook the onion, carrot, and parsnip, covered, until the onion is translucent.

To the contents of the soup kettle, add the cabbage, water, bouillon cubes, bay leaves, cumin, and sugar. Bring the liquid to the boil, reduce the heat, and simmer the vegetables, covered, for 30 minutes, or until they are tender. Season the soup to taste with salt and pepper. Serve it garnished with sour cream.

VARIATION: *this rather simple soup may be given quite an "air" by stirring into it, just before serving, 4 tablespoonfuls of blue cheese beaten with ⅓ cupful of light cream. Omit the sour cream garnish.*

CABBAGE SOUP
France

Yield: about 12 cups
Preparation: about 1¾ hours

Peasant fare which, served with honest bread and sweet butter, constitutes a complete meal.

---

6 cups water
6 vegetable or chicken bouillon cubes
1 small cabbage, shredded
1 medium-size carrot, scraped and cut in ½-inch rounds
1 rib celery, trimmed and chopped
1 large clove garlic, peeled and chopped fine
1 medium-size onion, peeled and sliced
1 medium-size white turnip, scraped and diced
1 bay leaf
½ teaspoon marjoram
4 peppercorns, crushed
½ teaspoon thyme
½ cup chopped parsley
1 tablespoon sugar
1 medium-size potato, peeled and grated

In a soup kettle, combine these ingredients, adding last the grated potato. Stir the mixture. Bring the liquid to the boil, reduce the heat, and simmer the vegetables, covered, for 1¼ hours.

1 (20-ounce) can red kidney beans, with their liquid
Salt
Pepper

Without draining the kidney beans, stir them into the soup. Adjust the seasoning to taste. Heat the soup to serving temperature.

CABBAGE SOUP
Russia

Yield: about 14 cups
Preparation: about 1½ hours

Shchi *is traditionally served with meat in it; if you are making stock for this recipe, add to it 1 pound of beef chuck in one piece and, after simmering it for 1½ hours, or until it is tender, remove and dice it. Reserve the diced meat and add it to the vegetables when you add the stock (see below). If you are using already prepared stock, prepare the recipe as written.*

4 tablespoons butter
1½ pounds cabbage, quartered, cored, and shredded
1 celeriac (celery root), scraped and cut into julienne
2 large onions, peeled and sliced thin
1 parsley root, scraped and cut into julienne

In a soup kettle, heat the butter and in it cook the cabbage, celeriac, onion, and parsley, stirring, until the onion is translucent. Reduce the heat and simmer the vegetables, covered, for 15 minutes.

8 cups Beef Stock *or* 6 (10½-ounce) cans beef broth
(Reserved diced beef)

Add the stock (and diced beef). Bring the liquid to the boil, reduce the heat, and simmer the vegetables, covered, for 20 minutes.

2 large potatoes, peeled and diced

Add the potatoes and continue simmering the mixture, covered, for 20 minutes, or until the potatoes are tender.

4 medium-size ripe tomatoes, peeled, seeded, and chopped
Salt
Pepper
Sour cream

Stir in the tomatoes. Cook the soup, covered, for 10 minutes. Season it to taste with salt and pepper. Serve it garnished with sour cream.

SAUERKRAUT SOUP
Poland

Yield: about 14 cups
Preparation: about 1¾ hours

Kapuśniak *is a popular native dish. Serve it with black bread.*

---

1 (1-pound) ham bone, cracked
1 medium-size onion, peeled and chopped
1 pound sauerkraut, drained (reserve the liquid)
1 tablespoon caraway seed (optional)
8 cups water

In a soup kettle, combine these five ingredients. Bring the liquid to the boil, reduce the heat, and simmer the mixture, uncovered, for 1 hour.

4 tablespoons bacon fat (or butter)
6 large mushrooms, sliced
1 small onion, peeled and chopped fine
4 tablespoons flour

In a skillet, heat the bacon fat and in it cook the mushrooms and onion, stirring, until the onion is golden. Stir in the flour and, over gentle heat, cook the mixture for a few minutes.

1 (10-ounce) package frozen mixed vegetables, fully thawed to room temperature
Salt
Pepper
Reserved sauerkraut juice (optional)

To the contents of the kettle, add the flour mixture, stirring until the soup is somewhat thickened and smooth. Add the vegetables and continue to simmer the soup for 12 minutes or until they are tender.

Remove and discard the ham bone. Season the soup to taste with salt, pepper, and, if desired, sauerkraut juice.

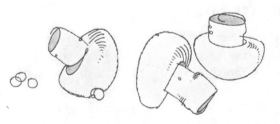

CARROT SOUP

Yield: about 8 cups
Preparation: about 1 hour

For a richer soup use Chicken Stock or canned broth in place of the water and bouillon cubes.

---

4 tablespoons butter
6 large carrots, scraped and chopped coarse
3 medium-size onions, peeled and chopped coarse
1 medium-size potato, peeled and chopped coarse

In a large saucepan, heat the butter and in it, over gentle heat, cook the vegetables, covered, for 20 minutes.

4 cups water
4 chicken bouillon cubes
2 bay leaves

Add these three ingredients, bring the liquid to the boil, reduce the heat, and simmer the mixture, covered, for 15 minutes, or until the vegetables are very tender. Discard the bay leaves.

In the container of a food processor or blender, whirl the mixture, 2 cupfuls at a time, until it is smooth.

2 cups milk, scalded
Salt
White pepper
¼ cup fine-chopped parsley

Stir in the milk. Season the soup to taste with salt and pepper. Serve it garnished with parsley.

VARIATION: *for* Carrot and Orange Soup, *in step two add the grated rind of 1 large orange; in step four in place of the milk use 2 cupfuls of strained fresh orange juice and omit the parsley.*

CARROT AND TOMATO SOUP

Yield: about 6 cups
Preparation: about 1 hour

---

6 tablespoons butter
6 large carrots, scraped and grated
2 ribs celery, chopped fine
1 large onion, peeled and grated

In a large saucepan, heat the butter and in it, over medium heat, cook the vegetables, stirring, until they just begin to brown.

3 medium-size ripe tomatoes,
peeled, seeded, and chopped

1 cup water

Add the water; bring the liquid to the boil, reduce the heat, and simmer the mixture, covered, for 25 minutes.

In the container of a food processor or blender, whirl the mixture until it is reduced to a smooth purée. Return the purée to the saucepan.

1 cup Chicken Stock *or* 1
(10½-ounce) can chicken
broth
2 cups tomato juice
1 teaspoon sugar
Salt
Pepper
Pesto genovese, page 241
(optional)

To the contents of the saucepan, add the stock, tomato juice, and sugar. Bring the soup to serving temperature. Season the soup to taste with salt and pepper.
When serving the soup, offer the *pesto* separately.

CORN CHOWDER
United States

Yield: about 8 cups
Preparation: about 45 minutes

A recipe from Aroostook County, Maine.

6 slices bacon, diced

In a large saucepan, render the bacon; drain it on absorbent paper and reserve it.

3 medium-size onions, peeled
and chopped

In the bacon fat, cook the onion until translucent.

3 large potatoes, peeled and
diced
2 cups water
1 teaspoon salt
¼ teaspoon pepper

Add the diced potato, stirring to coat it well. Add the water and salt and pepper. Bring the liquid to the boil, reduce the heat, and simmer the potato, covered, for 20 minutes, or until it is tender.

1 (20-ounce) can cream-style
corn
4 cups milk
Reserved diced bacon

Stir in the corn and milk. Heat the chowder thoroughly. Serve it garnished with the diced bacon.

DRIED CORN CHOWDER
United States

Yield: about 8 cups
Preparation: about 1 hour

A Pennsylvania Dutch recipe known locally as "winter corn chowder."

1½ cups dried corn, rinsed
4 cups Chicken Stock *or* 3 (10½-ounce) cans chicken broth

In a large saucepan, combine the dried corn and stock. Bring the liquid to the boil, remove the saucepan from the heat, and allow it to stand, covered, for 2 hours.

Return the liquid to the boil, reduce the heat, and simmer the corn, covered, for 45 minutes, or until it is tender.

6 slices bacon, diced

In a skillet, render the bacon; drain it on absorbent paper and reserve it.

3 medium-size onions, peeled and chopped

In the bacon fat, cook the onion until translucent.

4 cups milk
2 teaspoons sugar
Salt
Pepper
Reserved diced bacon

Add the onion and drippings to the contents of the saucepan. Add the milk and sugar. Heat the chowder thoroughly. Season it to taste with salt and pepper. Serve it garnished with the reserved diced bacon.

VARIATION: *if desired, 3 medium-size potatoes, peeled and diced, may be added in step two for the last 20 minutes of cooking.*

DILL PICKLE SOUP
Poland

Yield: about 8 cups
Preparation: about 50 minutes

This mildly piquant soup, served with black bread, makes a substantial meal.

---

6 medium-size dill pickles, diced and drained on absorbent paper

In a paper bag, combine the diced pickles and flour. Holding the bag closed, shake it vigorously to

4 tablespoons flour
4 tablespoons butter

5 cups Chicken Stock or 4
   (10½-ounce) cans chicken
   broth
½ teaspoon pepper

2 cups sour cream
   Salt
½ cup fine-chopped parsley

dredge the pickle evenly. In a large saucepan, heat the butter and in it cook the pickles, stirring them gently, for 5 minutes.

To the contents of the saucepan, add the stock and pepper. Bring the liquid to the boil, reduce the heat, and simmer the mixture, covered, for 30 minutes.

To the broth, add the sour cream, using a wire whisk to blend the soup well. Bring the soup to serving temperature. Adjust the seasoning to taste. Serve the soup garnished with the parsley.

EGGPLANT SOUP
Italy

Yield: about 8 cups
Preparation: about 45 minutes

For those who enjoy eggplant, I cannot recommend this soup too highly.

4 tablespoons olive oil
1 clove garlic, peeled and
   chopped fine
2 medium-size onions, peeled
   and chopped
3 tablespoons flour

1 large eggplant (about 2
   pounds), peeled and chopped
4 cups Chicken or Veal Stock
   or 3 (10½-ounce) cans
   chicken broth (you may use
   beef broth, if desired)
⅓ cup chopped parsley
½ teaspoon oregano

Salt
Pepper
Grated Parmesan cheese

In a large saucepan, heat the oil and in it cook the garlic and onion until translucent. Stir in the flour and, over gentle heat, cook the mixture for a few minutes.

To the contents of the saucepan, add the eggplant, stock, and seasonings. Bring the liquid to the boil, reduce the heat, and simmer the eggplant, covered, for 30 minutes.

(If desired, you may allow the soup to cool somewhat and then purée it in the container of a food processor or blender; bring the soup to serving temperature.)

Season the soup to taste with salt and pepper. When serving it, offer the grated cheese separately.

GREEN BEAN
AND HAM SOUP
United States

Yield: about 8 cups
Preparation: about 2½ hours

A Mennonite soup from Kansas.

---

1 (1-pound) ham bone with its meat
4 cups water

In a soup kettle, combine the ham bone and water. Bring the liquid to the boil, reduce the heat, and simmer the bone for 1½ hours.

Remove the meat from the bone, chop it, and return it to the broth; discard the bone.

2 cups cut-up green beans (cut in 1-inch pieces)
1 medium-size onion, peeled and sliced thin
1 large potato, peeled and diced
¼ cup fine-chopped parsley
½ teaspoon summer savory
½ teaspoon salt
¼ teaspoon pepper
1 cup light cream

To the broth, add these seven ingredients. Return the liquid to the boil, reduce the heat, and simmer the beans for 20 minutes, or until they are tender. Stir in the cream and bring the soup to serving temperature.

VARIATION: *for* Green Bean and Sorrel Soup, *in step three add 1 cupful of (fine-chopped, packed) sorrel leaves, which have been stemmed, rinsed, and dried on absorbent paper.*

LIMA BEAN SOUP
Colombia

Yield: about 10 cups
Preparation: about 3 hours

---

1 pound meaty beef bones, the fat removed
1 large carrot, scraped and sliced
1 medium-size onion, peeled and chopped
½ cup chopped parsley leaves

In a soup kettle, combine these six ingredients. Bring the liquid to the boil, reduce the heat, and simmer the beef bones, covered, for 2 hours, or until the meat falls from the bones; skim the surface as necessary.

1 (1-pound) can tomatoes, with their liquid	Remove the meat and the bones from the kettle. Chop the meat and reserve it. Discard the bones. Allow the broth to cool. Refrigerate the broth and the reserved meat overnight and the following day remove any solidified fat.
6 cups water	
1½ cups shelled Lima beans *or* 1 (10-ounce) package frozen Lima beans	Bring the broth to the boil, add the Lima beans, and cook them, covered, for 25 minutes, or until they are tender.
4 tablespoons cornstarch	In a small mixing bowl, blend together the cornstarch and milk. To the contents of the soup kettle, add the mixture, stirring constantly until the soup is thickened and smooth. Stir in the reserved meat. Season the soup to taste with salt and pepper.
⅓ cup milk	
Reserved meat	
Salt	
Pepper	

MINESTRONE
Italy

Yield: about 20 cups
Preparation: about 3¾ hours

There are nearly as many recipes for minestrone *as there are regions of Italy. The word, deriving from* minestra *("soup") and* -one *("big"), lives up to its meaning as a satisfying one-dish meal. It may or may not contain meat; it does contain pasta or rice or dried beans or peas for thickening. It is always served with grated cheese.*

4 tablespoons butter	In a soup kettle, heat the butter and oil and in the mixture, render the salt pork until crisp. With a slotted spoon, remove it to absorbent paper and reserve it. In the remaining fat, cook the onion until golden.
¼ cup olive oil	
¼ pound salt pork, diced	
2 large onions, peeled and sliced	
1 small cabbage, cored and shredded	To the onion, add the cabbage, carrot, and zucchini, stirring to coat them well; cook them for 5 minutes. ►
1 large carrot, scraped and sliced	
1 large zucchini, sliced	

1 cup red kidney beans, soaked overnight and drained

12 cups Beef Stock *or* 8 (10½-ounce) cans beef broth plus water to equal 12 cups

2 medium-size potatoes, peeled and diced

1 cup raw natural rice (preferably Italian)

2 cloves garlic, peeled and put through a press

¼ cup chopped parsley

½ teaspoon thyme

Salt

Pepper

Grated Parmesan cheese

Reserved diced salt pork

To the contents of the kettle, add the beans and stock. Bring the liquid to the boil, reduce the heat, and simmer the beans, covered, for 2 hours, or until they are tender.

Add the potato and rice and continue to simmer the soup, covered, for 30 minutes, stirring frequently.

Add the garlic, parsley, and thyme; continue to simmer the soup, covered, for 30 minutes. Season the *minestrone* to taste with salt and pepper. Offer the grated cheese and salt pork dice separately.

VARIATION: *for* Chilled Minestrone (*a Milanese summer favorite*), *stir into what remains of your initial serving of the soup grated Parmesan cheese to taste; over gentle heat, melt the cheese, stirring constantly. Allow the soup to cool and then chill it to the desired serving temperature; storing the soup in the refrigerator for longer than 2 days will weaken its flavor.*

ONION SOUP
France

Yield: about 8 cups
Preparation: about 45 minutes

This onion soup is said to have been a favorite of Napoleon III's.

6 tablespoons butter

2 pounds yellow onions, peeled and chopped

In a large saucepan, melt the butter and in it cook the onion until translucent.

In the container of a food processor or blender, purée the mixture. Return the purée to the saucepan.

3 cups dry white wine
1¼ cups Chicken Stock *or* 1
(10½-ounce) can chicken
broth
Salt
White pepper
2 cups grated Cantal cheese
or any hard grating cheese
Croutons, page 234

Into the purée, stir the wine and stock. Bring the soup to serving temperature. Season it to taste with salt and pepper. Stir the cheese into the soup and when it is melted serve the dish, garnished with croutons.

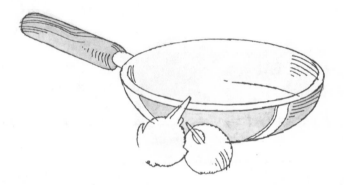

ONION SOUP
Switzerland

Yield: about 10 cups
Preparation: about 45 minutes

Traditionally made with Gruyère or Appenzeller cheese, this soup may also be made with Emmenthaler. It is best when made a day in advance; warm it in the top of a large double boiler over simmering water or over very gentle direct heat.

6 tablespoons sweet butter
8 large onions, peeled and sliced
thin
3 tablespoons flour

In a soup kettle, melt the butter and in it cook the onion until slightly golden. Stir in the flour and cook the mixture, stirring, for a few minutes. ►

4 cups milk, scalded
2 cups hot water

Gradually add first the milk and then the water, stirring constantly until the mixture is somewhat thickened and smooth.

2 cups grated cheese of your choice (see above)
1 tablespoon sugar
Generous grating of nutmeg
1 teaspoon salt
Pepper
Paprika
Croutons, page 234

To the broth, add the cheese, stirring until it is melted. Stir in the sugar, nutmeg, the salt, and pepper to taste. Simmer the soup over the lowest possible heat, covered, for 20 minutes. Serve the soup garnished with paprika; offer the croutons separately.

PARSNIP STEW
United States

Yield: about 10 cups
Preparation: about 1 hour

Really a chowder, using the traditional ingredients—pork, onion, and milk. A very good one-dish meal.

¼ pound salt pork, diced

In a flame-proof casserole, render the salt pork until it is crisp and golden. With a slotted spoon, remove it to absorbent paper and reserve it.

1 medium-size onion, peeled and chopped

In the remaining fat, cook the onion until golden.

4 medium-size parsnips, scraped and diced
3 medium-size potatoes, peeled and diced

Add the parsnips and potatoes, stirring to coat them well. Over medium heat, cook the mixture, stirring, for 5 minutes.

2 cups boiling water

Add the water and simmer the vegetables, covered, for 30 minutes, or until the parsnip is tender.

4 cups milk, scalded

Add the milk.

3 tablespoons soft butter
3 tablespoons flour
Salt

In a small mixing bowl combine the butter and flour. Using a fork, blend the mixture until it is smooth.

White pepper
Reserved diced salt pork
Dill weed

Add the *beurre manié* to the contents of the casserole, stirring constantly until the soup is thickened and smooth. Season the stew to taste with salt and pepper. Serve it garnished with the diced salt pork and a sprinkling of dill weed.

VARIATION: *for* Parsnip and Spinach Stew, *add, in step five, 1 cupful of fine-chopped (packed) fresh spinach leaves, which have been stemmed, rinsed, and dried on absorbent paper.*

PEASE POTAGE
England

Yield: about 9 cups
Preparation: about 40 minutes

The inspiration for the celebrated nursery rhyme:

Pease porridge hot,
Pease porridge cold,
Pease porridge in the pot
Nine days old.

---

3 tablespoons butter
1 leek, rinsed and chopped, the white part only
1 small onion, peeled and chopped
½ medium-size head Boston lettuce, rinsed, dried on absorbent paper, and chopped
1 tablespoon flour

In a large saucepan, heat the butter and in it cook the leek, onion, and lettuce until the lettuce is thoroughly wilted. Stir in the flour and, over gentle heat, cook the mixture for a few minutes.

¼ teaspoon cilantro
¼ teaspoon white pepper

Stir in the seasonings.

2½ cups fresh *or* frozen peas
4 cups Chicken Stock *or* 3 (10½-ounce) cans chicken broth
1 teaspoon sugar

To the contents of the saucepan, add the peas, stock, and sugar. Bring the liquid to the boil, reduce the heat, and simmer the peas, covered, for 20 minutes, or until they ▶

are very tender. With a slotted spoon, remove and reserve some of the peas for garnish.

In the container of a food processor or blender, whirl the mixture, 2 cupfuls at a time, until it is smooth. Return the soup to the saucepan.

1 cup light cream
2 tablespoons soft butter
  Salt
  Fine-chopped fresh chervil
  (optional)
  Reserved cooked peas

Stir in the cream and butter. Bring the soup to serving temperature and season it to taste with salt. Offer it garnished with chervil and the cooked peas.

VARIATION: *for* Cream of Pea and Spinach Soup (Potage Fontanges *—named for a mistress of Louis XIV's), omit the lettuce in step one and the cilantro in step two; add, in step three, ½ cupful of fine-chopped (packed) fresh spinach leaves, which have been stemmed, rinsed, and dried on absorbent paper.*

POTATO SOUP
France

Yield: about 16 cups
Preparation: about 1 hour

After dismissing American potatoes as food for livestock, Antoine-Auguste Parmentier, for whom this potage Parmentier *was named, survived on them for one year as a German prisoner. In 1779, once again on native soil, he wrote and was acclaimed for* Plants That Can Best Replace Cereals in Time of Famine, *which lauded the virtues of the lowly tuber. He then set out to popularize the potato and succeeded so well that, according to legend, the king himself sampled and succumbed to the delights of* pommes de terre. *Today the French prepare potatoes in more ways than, probably, any other nation.*

---

4 tablespoons butter
1 large carrot, scraped and cut in ½-inch rounds
3 ribs celery, chopped
6 leeks, rinsed and chopped, the white part only

In a soup kettle, heat the butter and in it cook the vegetables until the onion is translucent.

6 medium-size potatoes, peeled and chopped
Bouquet garni, page 2
8 cups water
8 chicken bouillon cubes (optional)

To the contents of the kettle, add these ingredients. Bring the liquid to the boil, reduce the heat, and simmer the vegetables, covered, for 30 minutes, or until the potato is very tender. Discard the *bouquet garni.*

In the container of a food processor or blender, whirl the mixture, 2 cupfuls at a time, until it is smooth. Transfer the purée to a large saucepan.

1 cup heavy cream
3 tablespoons soft butter
Salt
White pepper
Chopped parsley

Stir in the cream and butter. Bring the soup to serving temperature and season it to taste with salt and pepper. Garnish it with parsley.

VARIATIONS: *for a richer soup, in step two use 4 cupfuls of water and 4 cupfuls of Chicken Stock or 3 (10½-ounce) cans of chicken broth.* ►

In place of the parsley, garnish the soup with fine-chopped fresh mint leaves—as is done in Greece. Or with diced cucumber prepared from 2 medium-size cucumbers, peeled and seeded.

For Potato and Cabbage Soup: *add in step one, 1 small cabbage, quartered, cored, and shredded, the chopped leaves from 1 bunch of parsley, and 1 clove of garlic, peeled and chopped fine. Do not purée this soup.*

For Potato and Carrot Soup, *increase in step one the carrots to 6; add the zest of 1 small lemon, 1 clove of garlic, peeled and chopped fine, and ½ teaspoonful each of ground allspice and ground ginger. Complete the recipe as written.*

For Potato and Cheese Soup, *in step four add with the cream and butter ½ cupful of grated Gruyère cheese, stirring until it is melted; as a garnish, omit the parsley and offer grated Parmesan cheese separately.*

For Potato and Lamb Soup, *in step four after the cream and butter add 1½ cupfuls of diced cooked lamb.*

For Potato and Spinach Soup, *add in step two 1 (10-ounce) package fresh spinach, stemmed, rinsed, dried, and chopped, or 1 (10-ounce) package frozen chopped spinach.*

For Potato and Watercress Soup, *add in step four 1 bunch of watercress, stemmed, rinsed, dried, and chopped; omit the parsley.*

POTATO SOUP
United States

Yield: about 8 cups
Preparation: about 1 hour

A recipe from Aroostook County, Maine.

---

4 tablespoons butter 3 medium-size ribs celery, chopped 4 medium-size onions, peeled and sliced thin	In the top of a large double boiler, over direct heat, melt the butter and in it cook the celery and onion until translucent.

4 cups milk	Add the milk and, over simmering water, cook the mixture, covered, for 45 minutes.
3 large potatoes, peeled and diced	In boiling salted water to cover, cook the potato for 10 minutes. Drain and reserve it.
3 tablespoons butter 2 tablespoons flour	In a mixing bowl, blend the butter and flour until the mixture is smooth. Add the *beurre manié* to the contents of the double boiler, stirring until the mixture is thickened and smooth.
Reserved potato Salt Pepper Fine-chopped parsley	Stir in the potato. Season the soup to taste with salt and pepper. Over simmering water, allow it to cook, covered, for 10 minutes. Serve it garnished with parsley.

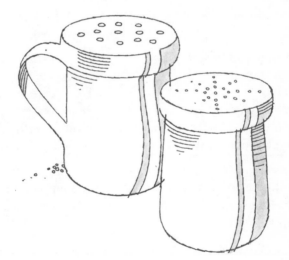

POTATO SOUP
United States

Yield: about 12 cups
Preparation: about 1 hour

A Pennsylvania Dutch recipe which may be served hot or chilled.

---

4 tablespoons butter
4 leeks, rinsed and chopped, the white part only
1 large onion, peeled and chopped

In a large saucepan, heat the butter and in it cook the leek and onion until they are translucent.

4 medium-size potatoes, peeled and sliced
4 cups Beef Stock *or* 3 (10½-ounce) cans beef broth

Add the potatoes and stock. Bring the liquid to the boil, reduce the heat, and simmer the potatoes, covered, for 25 minutes, or until they are very tender.

In the container of a food processor or blender, whirl the mixture, 2 cupfuls at a time, until it is smooth. Transfer it to a 5-quart casserole.

2 cups hot milk
2 cups hot cream
Salt
White pepper
2 bratwurst sausages, sliced thin *or* chopped chives

Stir in the milk and cream and bring the soup briefly to the boil. Season it to taste with salt and pepper. Serve the soup hot garnished with bratwurst slices or chilled garnished with chopped chives.

VARIATIONS: *for* Potato and Carrot Soup, *add in step two 1 cupful of grated raw carrot; serve the soup hot garnished with fine-chopped parsley.*

For Curried Potato Soup, *add in step one, 1 clove of garlic, peeled and chopped fine, and 1½ teaspoonfuls of curry powder. Complete the recipe as written, using chopped parsley as a garnish.*

POTATO AND KALE SOUP
Portuguese

Yield: about 14 cups
Preparation: about 45 minutes

Caldo verde *may be made with various green vegetables, although the potatoes and sausage remain constants. The Portuguese were among the first European peoples to make extensive use of potatoes.*

---

5 tablespoons olive oil
4 medium-size potatoes, peeled and sliced
8 cups water

In a soup kettle, heat the olive oil and in it stir the potato until it is well coated. Add the water, bring it to the boil, and cook the potato for 25 minutes, or until it is very tender.

¼ pound *chorizo or* other garlic-flavored smoked sausage

With the tines of a fork, prick the sausage in several places and, while the potato is cooking, simmer it over low heat for 15 minutes. Drain it on absorbent paper, slice it in ½-inch rounds, and reserve.

In the container of a food processor or blender, whirl the potato until it is reduced to a smooth purée. Return the purée to the soup kettle.

Reserved *chorizo*
1 pound fresh kale, rinsed, dried, and chopped, the woody stems removed
Salt
Pepper

To the contents of the soup kettle, add the reserved sausage. Stir in the kale, bring the mixture to the boil, reduce the heat, and simmer the greens, covered, for 5 minutes, or until they are tender. Season the soup to taste with salt and pepper.

VARIATION: *in place of the kale you may use 1 medium-size cabbage, cored and shredded, or 2 (10-ounce) packages of fresh spinach, rinsed, dried, and chopped, the woody stems removed, or 2 (10-ounce) packages of frozen chopped spinach.*

RICE AND PEA SOUP
Italy

Yield: about 10 cups
Preparation: about 1 hour

Risi e bisi *is a specialty of the Veneto region, said to have been eaten by the Doges of Venice as part of the Feast of St. Mark celebration. If desired, you may make the dish with 2 (10-ounce) packages frozen tiny peas, fully thawed to room temperature and added in step four for the last few minutes of cooking.*

⅛ pound salt pork, diced
Water

Boil the diced salt pork in water to cover for 10 minutes and drain.

3 tablespoons butter
2 tablespoons olive oil
1 medium-size onion, peeled and chopped

In a large saucepan, heat the butter and oil and in it fry the diced salt pork until crisp. Add the onion and cook it until translucent.

1 cup raw natural rice (preferably Italian)

Add the rice and, over gentle heat, cook it for 5 minutes.

8 cups Chicken Stock *or* 6 (10½-ounce) cans chicken broth

Add the broth and bring it to the boil.

1 pound peas, shelled
½ cup chopped parsley
Salt
Pepper
Grated Parmesan cheese

Into the boiling rice mixture, stir the peas. Cook the soup for 20 minutes, or until the rice and peas are tender. Stir in the parsley. Season the soup to taste with salt and pepper. Offer the grated cheese separately.

VARIATION: *for* Rice and Sausage Soup (*Italy*), *follow the recipe as written, omitting the peas but adding in step four 1 pound of Italian sweet sausage, which has been boiled for 10 minutes, drained, and cut in ½-inch rounds.*

SALSIFY SOUP
United States

Yield: about 6 cups
Preparation: about 45 minutes

This dish is called "Mock-oyster Soup" in its native Pennsylvania Dutch country.

Water
3 tablespoons vinegar
1¼ pounds salsify (oyster plant), scraped and sliced
Boiling salted water

To a large saucepan, add enough water to cover the salsify. Add the vinegar to the water and bring to the boil.
Cook the salsify, uncovered, for 3 minutes. Drain it. In a large saucepan, cook the salsify in 1 inch of boiling salted water for 20 minutes, or until it is tender. Reserve the salsify and its liquid.

3 tablespoons butter
1 small onion, peeled and chopped
3 tablespoons flour

In another large saucepan, heat the butter and in it cook the onion until translucent. Stir in the flour and, over gentle heat, cook the mixture for a few minutes.

1½ cups Chicken Stock *or* 1 (10½-ounce) can chicken broth plus water to equal 1½ cups
1½ cups milk
Reserved salsify and liquid

Gradually add first the stock and then the milk, stirring constantly until the mixture is thickened and smooth.
Add the salsify and its liquid.

(If desired, you may purée the mixture, 2 cupfuls at a time, in the container of a food processor or blender.)

Salt
Pepper
Fine-chopped parsley

Season the soup to taste with salt and pepper. Serve it garnished with parsley.

SWEET POTATO SOUP

Yield: about 10 cups
Preparation: about 50 minutes

2 ribs celery, trimmed and chopped
2 medium-size onions, peeled and chopped
3 medium-size sweet potatoes, peeled and chopped
4 cups water
4 beef bouillon cubes
1 bay leaf
1½ teaspoons tarragon

2 cups milk, scalded
Salt
White pepper
Chopped parsley

In a large saucepan, combine these seven ingredients. Bring the liquid to the boil, reduce the heat, and simmer the sweet potatoes, covered, for 30 minutes, or until they are very tender.

In the container of a food processor or blender, whirl the mixture, 2 cupfuls at a time, until it is smooth.

To the saucepan, together with the scalded milk, add the purée. Bring the soup to serving temperature. Season it to taste with salt and pepper. Serve it garnished with parsley.

WINTER SQUASH SOUP*

Yield: about 8 cups
Preparation: about 30 minutes

4 tablespoons butter
2 medium-size onions, peeled and chopped fine
4 tablespoons flour

Generous grating of nutmeg
2 cups Chicken Stock *or* 2 cups water to which 3 chicken bouillon cubes, crushed, have been added
4 cups milk

2 (10-ounce) packages frozen winter squash, fully thawed to room temperature
Salt
White pepper
Fine-chopped parsley

In a large saucepan, heat the butter and in it cook the onion until translucent. Stir in the flour and, over gentle heat, cook the mixture for a few minutes.

Stir in the nutmeg. Gradually add the stock and then the milk, stirring constantly until the mixture is thickened and smooth.

Add the squash and, over moderate heat, simmer the soup, covered, for 10 minutes. Season the soup to taste with salt and pepper. Serve it garnished with parsley.

HOT THIN SOUPS

Thin soups, admirable as first courses, stimulate the appetite but do not slake it. Clear thin soups are a bit fussier to make than thick or cream soups because clarifying them, if desired, is time consuming, albeit not difficult.

BARLEY SOUP
Austria

Yield: about 7 cups
Preparation: about 1½ hours

Gerstensuppe *is a popular first course in many Viennese homes.*

---

3 tablespoons butter
½ cup medium-size pearl barley
1 medium-size rib celery, diced
1 medium-size onion, peeled and chopped fine

1 tablespoon flour
6 cups hot Chicken or Vegetable Stock *or* 4 (10½-ounce) cans chicken broth plus water to equal 6 cups
½ cup heavy cream, scalded
Salt
Pepper

In a large saucepan, heat the butter and in it, over medium heat, cook the barley, celery, and onion, stirring, until the onion is translucent.

Into the contents of the saucepan, stir the flour. Gradually add the stock, stirring until the mixture is smooth. Bring the liquid to the boil, reduce the heat, and simmer the barley, covered, for 45 minutes, or until it is very tender. Just before serving, stir in the cream. Season the soup with salt and pepper to taste.

VARIATION: *for* Barley Soup with Meatballs (*a main-dish soup for a light meal*), *season and roll into small balls 1 pound of ground chuck. Brown the meatballs in a saucepan; remove and drain them on absorbent paper. Reserve them. In place of the butter, use the beef drippings to cook the barley, celery, and 3 large onions, peeled and chopped coarse. In place of the chicken or vegetable stock, use Beef Stock or broth. Simmer the soup as directed. Omit the cream. When the barley is cooked, add the reserved meatballs and simmer the soup for an additional 5 to 10 minutes. Season as directed.*

BARLEY
AND YOGURT SOUP
Turkey

Yield: about 6 cups
Preparation: about 1 hour

Middle Eastern soups are often made with yogurt, which lends a smooth consistency and a pleasant, slightly tart taste. The soup may be served hot or chilled.

2 tablespoons butter
2 medium-size onions, peeled and chopped fine

In a large saucepan, heat the butter and in it cook the onion until translucent.

½ cup medium-size pearl barley
4 cups Chicken Stock *or* 3 (10½-ounce) cans chicken broth

Add the barley and stock. Bring the liquid to the boil, reduce the heat, and simmer the barley, covered, for 35 minutes, or until it is tender.

⅓ cup chopped fresh mint *or* 1½ teaspoons dried mint
2 cups plain yogurt
Salt
White pepper
½ cup fine-chopped parsley

Away from the heat, stir in the mint and yogurt; reheat but do not allow the soup to return to the boil. Season it to taste with salt and pepper. Garnish it with the parsley.

BEAN SPROUT SOUP
China

Yield: about 8 cups
Preparation: about 2½ hours

1 (5-pound) fowl, disjointed
1 large onion, peeled and quartered
2 bay leaves
2 whole cloves
1 tablespoon sugar
1 tablespoon salt
Water

In a soup kettle, arrange the fowl, onion, and seasonings. Add water to cover by 1 inch. Bring the water to the boil, reduce the heat, and simmer the fowl, covered, for 1½ hours, or until it is very tender.

Remove the chicken; strain the broth. Discard the skin and bones of the chicken and cut the meat into thin julienne. Return it to the broth. Allow the broth to cool, refrigerate it overnight, and the following day remove any solidified fat.

3 tablespoons vegetable oil	In a skillet, heat the oil and in it cook the onion until it is golden. Add the bean sprouts and sprinkle the ginger over all. Cook the vegetables, stirring, for 5 minutes.
3 medium-size onions, peeled and chopped fine	
1½ cups bean sprouts (preferably fresh, but canned will do)	
2 teaspoons ground ginger	
	To the reheated broth, add the sprout mixture and cook for 10 minutes before serving.

BREAD SOUP

Yield: about 6 cups
Preparation: about 25 minutes

An old-fashioned recipe and a very effective digestive.

⅓ cup olive oil	In a saucepan, heat the oil and in it cook the garlic until it is golden. Discard the garlic and retain the oil.
3 cloves garlic, peeled and split	
4 cups Chicken Stock *or* 3 (10½-ounce) cans chicken broth	To the oil in the saucepan, add the stock and water. Bring the liquid to the boil.
2 cups water	
1 cup toasted bread crumbs	Stir in the bread crumbs. Simmer the mixture, covered, for 10 minutes.
3 eggs, beaten Salt Pepper Fine-chopped parsley	Into the gently boiling soup, whisk the eggs until they set in strands. Remove the soup from the heat and season it to taste with salt and pepper. Serve the soup garnished with parsley.

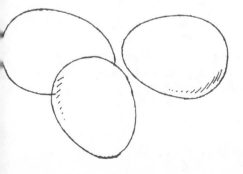

CELERY BROTH

Yield: about 6 cups
Preparation: about 1 hour

4 tablespoons butter 2 cups fine-chopped celery	In a saucepan, heat the butter and in it, over medium heat, cook the celery, covered, for 15 minutes.
6 cups Chicken Stock *or* 4 (10½-ounce) cans chicken broth plus water to equal 6 cups Salt White pepper	Add the stock, bring the liquid to the boil, reduce the heat, and simmer the celery, covered, for 30 minutes. Strain the liquid; use the cooked celery as a table vegetable and season the broth to taste with salt and pepper.

CELERY AND LEEK SOUP

Yield: about 6 cups
Preparation: about 30 minutes

4 tablespoons butter 6 leeks, rinsed and chopped, the white part only 4 tablespoons flour	In a large saucepan, heat the butter and in it cook the leeks, stirring, until they are limp. Stir in the flour and, over gentle heat, cook the mixture for a few minutes.
4 chicken bouillon cubes, crushed 4 cups milk	Into the contents of the saucepan, stir the crushed bouillon cubes. Gradually add the milk, stirring constantly until the mixture is thickened and smooth.
2 cups fine-diced celery Worcestershire sauce (optional) Salt Pepper Grated Parmesan cheese	Add the celery and, over gentle heat, simmer the soup, covered, for 20 minutes, or until the celery is tender-crisp. Season the soup to taste with salt and pepper. Serve it garnished with Parmesan cheese.

CHICKEN AND ORANGE CONSOMMÉ

Yield: about 7 cups
Preparation: about 20 minutes

The soup may be served hot or chilled.

---

4 cups Chicken Stock *or* 3 (10½-ounce) cans chicken broth
3 cups strained fresh orange juice
Salt
White pepper

In a saucepan, combine the stock and orange juice. Season the mixture to taste.

4 teaspoons cornstarch, mixed with ¼ cup cold water
6 orange slices, cut paper-thin and seeded

Add the cornstarch and, over high heat, bring the liquid to the boil, stirring constantly until the mixture is thickened and smooth. Serve the consommé garnished with orange slices.

VARIATIONS: *for* Jellied Chicken and Orange Consommé, *in step two omit the cornstarch, but sprinkle 2 envelopes of unflavored gelatin over the contents of the saucepan and allow it to soften for 5 minutes; over gentle heat, dissolve the gelatin, stirring; add the grated rind of 1 medium-size orange. Allow the consommé to cool and then chill it for at least 6 hours.*

For Chicken and Tarragon Consommé,* *in step one increase the chicken stock to 5 cupfuls or 4 (10½-ounce) cans of chicken broth and reduce the orange juice to 2 cupfuls; in step two, before the addition of the cornstarch, add 2 tablespoonfuls of chopped fresh tarragon, or 1 tablespoonful of dried tarragon; add the cornstarch and simmer the mixture, covered, for 5 minutes; strain it into a second saucepan and garnish as written. (Note: this variation may also be served either hot or cold.)*

CONSOMMÉ

Yield: about 10 cups
Preparation: about 5½ hours

3 pounds boneless soup beef, cut in 1-inch cubes
1 pound beef bones, cracked
1 pound veal knuckle, cracked
1 chicken carcass (left over from roast chicken)
1 tablespoon salt
12 cups water

In a soup kettle, combine these six ingredients. Bring the liquid to the boil slowly, reduce the heat, and simmer the meat, covered, for 4 hours.

2 carrots, scraped and chopped
2 ribs celery, chopped, with their leaves
1 clove garlic, peeled and split
1 medium-size onion, peeled and quartered
6 sprigs parsley
3 bay leaves
6 peppercorns

To the contents of the soup kettle, add the vegetables and seasonings. Continue to simmer the ingredients, uncovered, for 1 hour.

Strain the broth through a double thickness of cheesecloth. Allow it to cool. Discard the residue (most of the food value will have been cooked out of both meats and vegetables). Store the broth in the refrigerator. Do not remove the layer of fat until you are ready to use the broth (it provides a seal for storing).

When the consommé is to be used, clarify the broth, page 247.

DOUBLE CONSOMMÉ

Yield: about 8 cups
Preparation: about 1½ hours

6 cups Beef or Chicken Stock *or* 5 (10½-ounce) cans beef or chicken broth
1 pound lean ground beef *or* chicken

In a saucepan, combine these five ingredients. Bring the liquid to the boil, reduce the heat, and simmer the mixture, covered, for 1 hour.

1 carrot, scraped and sliced
  thin
1 rib celery, chopped fine
1 leek, rinsed and sliced thin,
  the white part only

½ cup dry sherry or Madeira
  wine
  Strained juice of 1 small
  lemon
  Salt

Strain the broth, discarding the residue. Allow it to cool, and store the broth in the refrigerator. Do not remove the layer of fat until you are ready to use the broth (it provides a seal for storing).

When the consommé is to be used, clarify the broth, page 247. Stir in the wine and lemon juice; adjust the seasoning to taste.

EGG CONSOMMÉ
Italy

Yield: about 6 cups
Preparation: about 15 minutes

Zuppa alla Pavese is a well-known first course throughout Italy. It is light, delicate, and elegant; and its success depends upon the quality of the stock (if you use canned chicken broth, I recommend that you boil it down to the quantity required—see the ingredient column, below).

---

6 cups Chicken Stock (or Veal,
  if you wish) *or* 6
  (10½-ounce) cans chicken
  broth reduced to 6 cups
3 tablespoons fine-chopped
  parsley

3 eggs, beaten
  Salt
  White pepper
  Grated Parmesan cheese

In a saucepan, combine the stock and parsley. Bring the stock to a gentle boil.

Stir in the egg and cook it, stirring constantly, until it is set. Season the soup to taste with salt and pepper. Serve it garnished with grated cheese.

VARIATION: *in individual oven-proof dishes, break an egg, leaving the yolk intact; after the stock-parsley mixture comes to a boil, ladle it over the egg. Place the dishes in a preheated 400° oven for 5 minutes, or until the egg is just set. Season as directed and serve the soup garnished with Cheese Toasts, page 234.*

EGG-DROP SOUP
China

Yield: about 6 cups
Preparation: about 20 minutes

6 cups Chicken Stock *or* 5 (10½-ounce) cans chicken broth
2 scallions, minced, with as much of the green as is crisp
1 tablespoon soy sauce
1 tablespoon rice vinegar *or* lemon juice
¼ teaspoon pepper
½ teaspoon salt

In a large saucepan, combine these six ingredients. Bring the liquid to the boil and reduce the heat to simmer.

2 tablespoons cornstarch in ¼ cup cold water
3 eggs, beaten

Into the simmering broth, stir the cornstarch mixture; continue stirring until the broth is thickened and clear. Stir in the eggs. As soon as they have set, serve the soup.

VARIATIONS: *1 cupful of cooked green peas or ½ cupful of fresh chopped (tightly packed) spinach, which has been stemmed, rinsed, and dried on absorbent paper, may be added in step one.*

EGG
AND LEMON SOUP
Greece

Yield: about 6 cups
Preparation: 30 minutes

Soupa avgolemono, *as Greek as Delphi's oracle, will not "hold"; the prepared broth and egg mixture should be combined only at the time of serving.*

6 cups Chicken Stock *or* 5 (10½-ounce) cans chicken broth
⅓ cup raw natural rice
1 teaspoon salt
¼ teaspoon white pepper

In a large saucepan, bring the stock to the boil. Add the rice and seasonings, stirring to prevent the rice from sticking. Reduce the heat and simmer the rice, covered, for 15 minutes, or until it is tender.

3 eggs
    Strained juice of 1
    medium-size lemon

    Fine-chopped parsley
    (optional)

Meanwhile, beat the eggs with the lemon juice until the mixture is light.

To serve, stir, 1 tablespoonful at a time, ½ cup of the simmering broth into the egg mixture. Then, away from the heat, stir all of the egg mixture into the broth. Serve the soup at once, garnished, if desired, with chopped parsley.

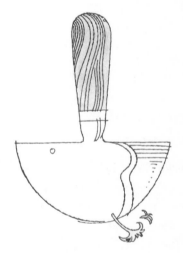

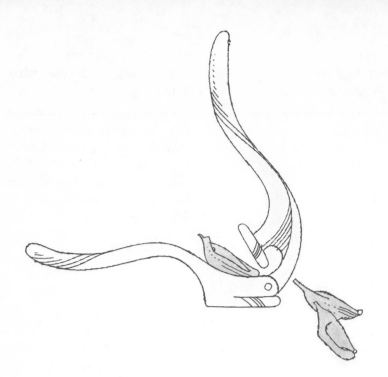

GARLIC SOUP
Spain

Yield: about 9 cups
Preparation: about 1½ hours

Garlic is one of our most ancient medicinals; the Greeks had used it as a digestive as well as for other ills before the Romans fell under its heady spell. They, in turn, brought it to Spain where at once it became integral to Spanish cooking. In 1330, however, King Alfonso XI, who apparently had a very sensitive nose, banished from his court not only garlic itself, but also any knight who smelled of it.

½ cup olive oil
1 large bulb garlic (about 20 cloves), the cloves peeled and sliced lengthwise

In a skillet, heat the oil and in it cook the garlic until it is golden. Remove it with a slotted spoon and reserve it.

Slices of stale white bread

Off the heat, dip each slice of bread in the hot oil, turning it once. Then, in the skillet, sauté each slice until it is golden and crisp. Reserve.

Reserved garlic
4 cups water

In a large saucepan, combine the garlic, water, and stock. Bring the

4 cups Beef Stock *or* 3 (10½-ounce) cans beef broth	liquid to the boil, reduce the heat, and simmer the garlic for 45 minutes.
	Strain and reserve the broth. In the container of a food processor or blender, whirl the garlic until it is reduced to a smooth purée. (Add a little of the broth to facilitate this step.) Return the purée to the broth.
6 egg yolks, beaten Salt White pepper	To 2 cupfuls of the broth, add the egg yolks, stirring vigorously. Away from the heat, beat the egg mixture into the remaining broth. Season the soup to taste with salt and pepper. Reheat the soup but do not allow it to boil.
Reserved bread slices	In each soup plate put a slice of bread; over it, ladle the soup.

VARIATION: *omit the sautéed bread but reserve the flavored oil from step one; in step six omit the egg yolks, but thicken the soup with 4 tablespoonfuls of cornstarch mixed with ½ cupful of water; when serving the soup, fry 6 eggs in the reserved oil, arrange them in individual plates, and ladle the soup over them.*

GARLIC SOUP*

Yield: about 6 cups
Preparation: about 1 hour

6 tablespoons butter 1 medium-size bulb garlic (15 to 20 cloves), peeled and chopped coarse 1 medium-size bunch parsley, the stems removed	In a large saucepan or soup kettle, heat the butter and in it, over gentle heat, cook the garlic and parsley, stirring often, until the parsley is wilted.
4 tablespoons flour 4 bouillon cubes, crushed 1 teaspoon powdered cumin (optional)	Stir in the flour, bouillon powder, and cumin. Over gentle heat, cook the mixture for a few minutes. ►

4 cups water	Gradually add the water, stirring constantly until the mixture is thickened and smooth. Over gentle heat, simmer the soup, covered, for 30 minutes; stir it often.
	In the container of a food processor or blender, whirl the mixture, 2 cupfuls at a time, until it is smooth. Return it to the saucepan.
2 cups milk, scalded Salt White pepper	Bring the soup to serving temperature. Add the milk, stirring to blend the soup well. Season it to taste with salt and pepper.

GREEN PEA SOUP
England

Yield: about 9 cups
Preparation: about 40 minutes

This recipe is said to have been a favorite of Queen Victoria's.

3 cups shelled green peas *or* 2 (10-ounce) packages frozen peas, fully thawed to room temperature 6 cups Beef or Chicken Stock *or* 4 (10½-ounce) cans beef or chicken broth plus water to equal 6 cups ¼ cup chopped fresh mint leaves ½ cup chopped parsley leaves 4 scallions, chopped, with as much green as is crisp 2 teaspoons sugar	In a large saucepan, combine these six ingredients. Bring the liquid to the boil, reduce the heat, and simmer the peas, covered, for 20 minutes, or until they are very tender. In the container of a food processor or blender, whirl the mixture, 2 cupfuls at a time, until it is smooth. Return it to the saucepan.
2 tablespoons butter Salt Pepper Croutons, page 234	Bring the soup to serving temperature. Stir in the butter. Season the soup to taste with salt and pepper. Serve it garnished with croutons.

VARIATIONS: *for* Cream of Green Pea Soup, *in step one omit the mint leaves; use 5 cupfuls of Chicken Stock or 4 (10½-ounce) cans of chicken broth; add to the soup, after whirling it in the food processor, 1 cupful of cream (heavy or light, as your fancy dictates).*

For Green Pea Soup with Watercress, *in step one omit the mint leaves but add 1 bunch of watercress, rinsed, dried, and chopped, the woody stems removed.*

KIDNEY SOUP
China

Yield: about 8 cups
Preparation: about 1 hour

1½ pounds pork kidneys Salted water	Halve the kidneys lengthwise, remove the fat, and soak them for 2 hours in cold salted water. Drain and parboil them for 1 minute in salted water. Drain and chop them coarse; reserve them.
2 tablespoons vegetable oil Reserved kidneys ¼ cup diced ginger root	In a *wok,* heat the oil and, when it starts to smoke, add to it the kidneys and ginger. Stir-fry them for 1 minute.
2 tablespoons rice vinegar 1 tablespoon soy sauce ½ teaspoon salt	Add the seasonings and continue to stir-fry the kidneys until they just begin to brown.
½ cup rice wine *or* whisky 5½ cups water	Add the rice wine and water. Bring the liquid to the boil, reduce the heat, and gently simmer the kidneys for 10 minutes.
1 tablespoon cornstarch mixed with ½ cup water	Add the cornstarch and water mixture to the contents of the *wok,* stirring until the soup is slightly thickened.

OATMEAL SOUP
Mexico

Yield: about 8 cups
Preparation: about 40 minutes

1⅓ cups quick-cooking rolled oats

Sprinkle the rolled oats evenly over a baking sheet and toast them in a 350° oven for 10 minutes, or until they are golden. Reserve them.

6 tablespoons butter
3 large cloves garlic, peeled and chopped fine
1 large onion, peeled and chopped fine
2 large ripe tomatoes, peeled, seeded, and chopped
6 cups Chicken Stock *or* 4 (10½-ounce) cans chicken broth plus water to equal 6 cups

In a large saucepan, combine these five ingredients. Bring the liquid to the boil, reduce the heat, and simmer the mixture, covered, for 20 minutes.

Reserved rolled oats
Salt
Pepper

Into the contents of the saucepan, stir the rolled oats. Continue to simmer the soup, stirring often, for 6 minutes, or until the oats are tender. Season the soup to taste with salt and pepper.

MUSHROOM SOUP

Yield: about 8 cups
Preparation: about 45 minutes

---

1 pound button mushrooms

Remove the stems from the mushrooms and chop them fine. Reserve the tops.

7 cups Beef or Chicken, or Veal Stock *or* 5 (10½-ounce) cans broth of your choice plus water to equal 7 cups

In a large saucepan, combine the mushroom stems and stock. Bring the liquid to the boil, reduce the heat, and simmer the mixture, covered, for 30 minutes.

Strain the broth through cheese-cloth and discard the residue.

Salt
White pepper
Dry sherry (optional)
Reserved mushroom tops

Season the soup to taste with salt, pepper, and sherry. Serve it garnished with a few mushroom tops. (Reserve any remaining mushroom tops for another recipe.)

VARIATION: *for* Jellied Mushroom Soup, *add to the strained broth in step three, 3 envelopes of unflavored gelatin, softened for 5 minutes in ½ cupful of cold water, stirring to dissolve the gelatin. Allow the soup to cool before chilling it for at least 6 hours, or until it is thoroughly set; garnish it with chopped parsley.*

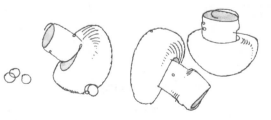

MUSHROOM SOUP
WITH BARLEY
United States

Yield: about 8 cups
Preparation: about 50 minutes

3 tablespoons butter
1 medium-size carrot, scraped and sliced thin
1 large rib celery, trimmed and chopped
1 clove garlic, peeled and chopped
1 medium-size onion, peeled and chopped

In a large saucepan, heat the butter and in it cook the vegetables until the onion is translucent. ►

1 pound mushrooms, trimmed and sliced thin

Add the mushrooms and cook them, stirring gently, until they are well coated with butter. (More butter may be added if necessary.)

6 cups Chicken or Veal Stock or 5 (10½-ounce) cans chicken broth or 6 cups water plus 8 chicken bouillon cubes
½ cup medium-size pearl barley
Salt
Pepper

Add the stock and barley. Bring the liquid to the boil, reduce the heat, and simmer the soup, covered, for 35 minutes, or until the barley is tender. Season it to taste with salt and pepper.

MUSTARD GREEN AND BEAN-THREAD SOUP
China

Yield: about 10 cups
Preparation: about 1 hour

A Szechuan delicacy.

½ pound lean pork, cut in fine julienne
1 teaspoon rice wine
1 teaspoon oriental sesame seed oil
2 teaspoons soy sauce

In a mixing bowl, combine and blend the pork with the rice wine, sesame seed oil, and soy sauce; allow it to marinate for 30 minutes.

1 tablespoon vegetable oil

In a *wok,* heat the oil and in it, over high heat, cook the pork and its marinade for 3 minutes. With a slotted spoon, remove the meat and reserve it.

6 cups Chicken Stock *or* 4
　(10½-ounce) cans chicken
　broth plus water to equal 6
　cups
1 (10-ounce) package frozen
　mustard greens, fully
　thawed to room
　temperature
1½ teaspoons very fine-chopped
　ginger root

½ ounce bean-thread noodles,
　soaked for 5 minutes in cold
　water and drained
1 medium-size cucumber,
　peeled and cut in 2-inch
　strips
　Reserved pork
　Soy sauce
　Thin-sliced scallions

To the contents of the *wok,* add the
stock and bring it to the boil. At
once add the mustard greens and
ginger. Over high heat, cook the
mustard greens, covered, for 20
minutes, or until they are just tender.

Add the bean threads, cucumber,
and reserved pork. Over medium
heat, cook the soup, uncovered, for
3 minutes.
Season the soup to taste with soy
sauce. Serve it garnished with scallions.

OKRA SOUP
United States

Yield: about 6 cups
Preparation: about 45 minutes

From our southland comes this simple, refreshing soup.

4 tablespoons butter
1 pound okra, rinsed, trimmed,
　and cut in ½-inch rounds
2 medium onions, peeled and
　sliced thin

2 large ripe tomatoes, peeled,
　seeded, and chopped
4 cups Chicken Stock *or* 3
　(10½-ounce) cans chicken
　broth
1 tablespoon chili powder
　Salt
　Pepper

In a large saucepan, heat the butter
and in it cook the okra and onion
until the onion is translucent. Stir
the vegetables often.

To the contents of the saucepan add
these three ingredients. Bring the
liquid to the boil, reduce the heat,
and simmer the vegetables, covered,
for 20 minutes. Season the soup to
taste with salt and pepper.

ONION SOUP
France

Yield: about 12 cups
Preparation: about 50 minutes

The traditional recipe.

---

2 tablespoons sweet butter
2 tablespoons olive oil
1½ pounds yellow onions, peeled and sliced thin

In a soup kettle heat the butter and olive oil. Add the onion and cook it over gentle heat, stirring occasionally, until it is golden.

3 tablespoons flour
1 teaspoon salt

Stir in the flour and salt and continue to cook the onion for 3 minutes.

8 cups Beef Stock *or*
6 (10½-ounce) cans beef broth
Salt
Pepper

Add the stock and simmer the soup, partially covered, for 30 minutes. Adjust the seasoning, to taste.

(¼-inch) slices of French bread
Olive oil

On a baking sheet, toast the bread slices at 300° for 20 minutes. Brush both sides with olive oil and bake them 10 minutes longer.

¾ cup grated Parmesan cheese
¾ cup grated Gruyère cheese

In a mixing bowl, toss together the cheeses.

To serve the soup, arrange two slices of the bread in the bottom of each warmed plate; over each slice, sprinkle 2 tablespoonfuls of cheese. Ladle the soup over the bread.

OYSTER STEW
United States

Yield: about 9 cups
Preparation: about 30 minutes

So simple, so good, so elegant!

---

6 tablespoons butter
¾ teaspoon Worcestershire sauce
1 teaspoon celery salt

In a saucepan, heat the butter. Stir in the Worcestershire sauce and celery salt. Over gentle heat, cook the mixture, stirring for a few minutes.

| 1½ pints shucked oysters, with their liquid | Add the oysters, and simmer them for about 2 minutes or until their edges begin to curl. |
| 6 cups hot milk *or* half-and-half *or* light cream
Salt
White pepper
Dry sherry (optional) | Add the milk. Season the stew to taste with salt, pepper, and sherry. |

VARIATIONS: *add 2 medium-size carrots, scraped and sliced very thin, to the seasoned butter in step one; cook them, covered, until they are tender. Two ribs celery, chopped very fine, or 2 medium-size onions, peeled and chopped fine, may be treated the same way. If desired, you may use all three vegetables.*

For Oyster and Artichoke Stew, *add in step two before the oysters 1 (9-ounce) package of frozen artichoke hearts, which have been cooked according to the directions on the package, drained, and chopped.*

For Oyster and Spinach Stew, *add in step two before the oysters 1 cupful of chopped (packed) spinach leaves, which have been washed, dried, and stemmed.*

SCALLOP STEW*

Yield: about 6 cups
Preparation: about 30 minutes

3 tablespoons butter 1 small onion, peeled and grated	In a saucepan, heat the butter and in it cook the onion for a few minutes.
1 pound sea scallops, quartered	Add the scallops and, over gentle heat, cook them for 5 minutes.
4 cups milk *or* 2 cups milk plus 2 cups light cream Salt White pepper 2 tablespoons soft butter Fine-chopped parsley *or* dill weed	Add the milk, bring the mixture to the simmer, and cook it gently, uncovered, for 10 minutes, or until the scallops are firm but still tender. Season the stew to taste with salt and pepper. Put a little butter in each cup or bowl, ladle the stew over it, and garnish it with parsley or dill.

SPINACH SOUP*

Yield: about 6 cups
Preparation: about 30 minutes

My adaptation of a very old English recipe.

---

2 (10-ounce) packages fresh spinach, rinsed and shaken dry, the woody stems removed *or* 2 (10-ounce) packages frozen chopped spinach, fully thawed to room temperature
5 cups water
1½ teaspoons salt
¼ teaspoon pepper

⅓ cup strained lemon juice
2 eggs, well beaten
Sour cream (optional)

In a large saucepan, combine these four ingredients. Bring the liquid to the boil, reduce the heat, and simmer the spinach, covered, for 12 minutes.

Allow the broth to cool to lukewarm. Whirl it, 2 cupfuls at a time, in the container of a food processor or blender. Return it to the saucepan.

Add the lemon juice and egg. Over gentle heat, warm the soup; do not let it boil. If desired, garnish each portion with 1 tablespoonful of sour cream.

VARIATION: *for a light* Sorrel Soup, *use, in place of the spinach, 1 pound of fresh sorrel leaves, stemmed, rinsed, and shaken dry. (Because sorrel is more flavorful than spinach, you will not need quite as large a quantity.)*

PORK AND WATERCRESS SOUP
China

Yield: about 9 cups
Preparation: about 40 minutes

I especially enjoy this Chinese soup, quickly made, visually appealing, and subtly seasoned.

½ pound lean pork, cut in fine julienne
4 cups water

In a *wok* or large saucepan, combine the pork and water. Bring the liquid to the boil, reduce the heat, and simmer the pork for 10 minutes.

1 large rib celery, diced	To the contents of the *wok,* add
1 medium-size onion, peeled and chopped fine	these three ingredients. Continue to simmer the mixture for 10 minutes.
4 cups stock of your choice *or* 3 (10½ -ounce) cans of beef or chicken broth	
1 bunch watercress, rinsed, dried, and chopped, the woody stems removed Salt Pepper	Add the watercress and bring the soup to the boil. Season it to taste with salt and pepper.

RICE SOUP
Greece

Yield: about 7 cups
Preparation: about 35 minutes

6 cups Beef or Chicken Stock *or* 4 (10½ -ounce) cans beef or chicken broth plus water to equal 6 cups	In a saucepan, combine the stock and rice. Cook the rice, covered, for 25 minutes, or until it is very tender.
1 cup raw natural rice (preferably Italian)	In the container of a food processor or blender, whirl the mixture, 2 cupfuls at a time, until it is smooth. Transfer it to a saucepan.
3 egg yolks, beaten	In a mixing bowl, using a rotary
1 cup hot milk	beater, blend the egg yolks and
2 tablespoons soft butter	milk. Stir the mixture into the rice purée. Stir in the butter.
Salt	Bring the soup to serving tempera-
White pepper	ture; do not allow it to boil. Season
Fine-chopped parsley	it to taste with salt and pepper and garnish it with parsley.

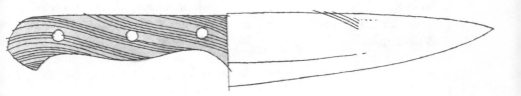

STRACCIATELLA
Italy

Yield: about 7 cups
Preparation: 30 minutes

This classic of Italian cuisine is often a first course in my home.

---

3 eggs ¼ cup semolina flour ⅓ cup fresh-grated Parmesan cheese ½ teaspoon salt	In a mixing bowl, combine these four ingredients and, with a rotary beater, blend them thoroughly.
1 cup Beef Stock *or* 1 (10½-ounce) can beef broth	Gradually add the stock, stirring to blend the mixture well. Transfer it to a large saucepan.
6 cups Beef Stock *or* 4 (10½-ounce) cans beef broth plus ½ cup boiling water	Into the contents of the saucepan, stir the additional boiling broth, beating the mixture with a whisk. When the egg breaks into strands, the soup is cooked and should be served at once.

CLEAR TOMATO SOUP*

Yield: about 8 cups
Preparation: about 1 hour

Because this soup is made with canned tomatoes, you can enjoy it year-round. The soup may be served hot or chilled.

---

1 tablespoon butter 1 tablespoon olive oil 1 large onion, peeled and chopped 2 tablespoons flour	In a large saucepan, heat the butter and oil; add the onion and cook it until translucent. Stir in the flour and, over gentle heat, cook the mixture for a few minutes.
4 cups water 6 chicken bouillon cubes 1 large rib celery, chopped, with its leaves 1 (28-ounce) can tomatoes, with their liquid 2 teaspoons sugar 1 teaspoon basil 1 bay leaf	Gradually add the water, stirring constantly until the mixture is slightly thickened and smooth. Add the bouillon cubes, celery, tomato, and seasonings. Bring the mixture to the boil, reduce the heat, and simmer it, covered, for 30 minutes. Strain the soup and discard the residue.

Strained juice of 1 small
lemon *or* lime
1 tablespoon Worcestershire
sauce
Few drops of Tabasco sauce
Salt
Croutons of your choice, pages
234–35 *or* fine-chopped
parsley

Season with the lemon juice and Worcestershire sauce and to taste with Tabasco sauce and salt. Serve it hot garnished with croutons or chilled garnished with parsley.

VARIATIONS: *for Clear Tomato and Celery Soup, in step three add 3 large ribs of celery, diced and cooked until translucent in 3 tablespoonfuls of butter.*

For Clear Tomato and Onion Soup, in step three add 3 large onions, peeled, chopped fine, and cooked until just golden in 3 tablespoonfuls of butter.

Vary the seasonings: in step two, omit the basil and in its place use 2 tablespoonfuls of dill weed or tarragon or a generous pinch of saffron.

For Jellied Tomato Soup, in step three add 2½ envelopes of unflavored gelatin softened for 5 minutes in ½ cupful of cold water; stir until the gelatin is dissolved. Chill the soup for at least 6 hours. A pleasant variation on this jellied soup is the addition in step three of 2 medium-size cucumbers or zucchini, which have been seeded, diced, and cooked for 2 minutes in 2 tablespoonfuls of butter. Use fine-chopped parsley and paper-thin lemon slices for garnish.

VEGETABLE SOUP
China

Yield: about 6 cups
Preparation: about 30 minutes

The Chinese way with vegetables.

5 cups Chicken Stock *or* 4
(10½-ounce) cans chicken
broth
2 medium-size carrots, scraped
and cut in fine julienne 1½
inches long

In a saucepan, combine these ingredients. Bring the liquid to the boil and cook the vegetables, covered, for 10 minutes, or until they are tender-crisp. Reduce the heat to low in order not to overcook them. ▶

½ cup peas
4 scallions, trimmed and sliced thin, with as much of the green as is crisp
½ cup fine-chopped (lightly packed) spinach leaves, which have been stemmed, rinsed, and dried on absorbent paper
Pinch of summer savory

Salt
Pepper
Fine-chopped cilantro *or* parsley

Season the soup to taste with salt and pepper. Serve it garnished with cilantro.

ZUCCHINI SOUP

Yield: about 8 cups
Preparation: about 40 minutes

1 tablespoon butter
1 small onion, peeled and chopped

In a large saucepan, heat the butter and in it cook the onion until translucent.

3 large zucchini, seeded and cut in ½-inch pieces
1 bay leaf
3 sprigs parsley
½ teaspoon thyme
6 cups Vegetable Stock *or* 6 cups water plus 6 envelopes vegetable bouillon powder

To the contents of the saucepan, add the zucchini, seasonings, and stock. Bring the liquid to the boil, reduce the heat, and simmer the zucchini, uncovered, for 10 minutes. Discard the bay leaf and parsley.

2 eggs, beaten
Generous grating of nutmeg
Salt
Pepper
Cheese Toasts, page 234

Into the beaten egg, whisk 1 cup of the broth. Then add the egg mixture to the soup, stirring vigorously. Season the soup to taste with nutmeg, salt, and pepper. Serve it with cheese toasts.

CHILLED AND JELLIED SOUPS

Before I became caught up in the making of soups (and the consuming of them), the idea of chilled soups seemed somewhat strange and that of jellied soups downright grotesque, but now warm-season meals at my home are more often than not introduced by them. As you will note from recipes in other sections of the book, many soups do not have to be made purposely as "chilled"; in the same way, you may gel any soup you wish, albeit you will enjoy most gelling clear soups. To do so, you need only remember that 1 package of unflavored gelatin will gel 2 to 2½ cupfuls of liquid, depending upon the degree of firmness you desire.

Suggestions for chilling and serving jellied soups appear on page 4.

CHILLED BEET AND BUTTERMILK SOUP

Yield: about 10 cups
Preparation: about 1 hour

You may use 2 (1-pound) cans of beets if you wish; use the beet liquid as part of the 3 cups of water.

---

8 large beets, peeled and grated
1 large onion, peeled and chopped coarse
3 cups water
3 bouillon cubes
¼ teaspoon celery seed
¼ teaspoon ground cloves

In a large saucepan, combine these six ingredients. Bring the liquid to the boil, reduce the heat, and simmer the mixture, covered, for 40 minutes.

In the container of a food processor or blender, whirl the mixture, 2 cupfuls at a time, until it is smooth.

4 cups buttermilk
Salt
Pepper
Chopped parsley
Sour cream (optional)

In a mixing bowl, combine and blend the beet mixture with the buttermilk. Adjust the seasoning to taste. Chill the soup for at least 4 hours.
Serve the soup in chilled bowls, garnished with a generous sprinkling of parsley and, if desired, a dollop of sour cream.

CHILLED BUTTERMILK SOUP
Denmark

Yield: about 5 cups
Preparation: about 20 minutes

You might try this soup as a cool and refreshing summer dessert.

---

2 eggs
¼ cup sugar
Pinch of salt

In a small mixing bowl, beat the eggs, sugar, and salt until the mixture is light. ▶

1 quart buttermilk
1 teaspoon vanilla extract

Strained juice and grated rind of 1 medium-size lemon
Whipped *or* sour cream

With a rotary beater, blend in the buttermilk and vanilla extract.

Stir in the lemon juice and rind. Chill the soup for at least 4 hours. Serve the soup garnished with whipped or sour cream.

CHILLED CARROT AND YOGURT SOUP

Yield: about 8 cups
Preparation: about 40 minutes

The humble carrot achieves apotheosis!

6 large carrots, scraped and sliced thin
3 cups Chicken Stock *or* 2 (10½-ounce) cans chicken broth

In a saucepan, combine the carrots and stock. Bring the stock to the boil and cook the carrots, covered, for 20 minutes, or until they are very tender. Strain them and reserve the carrots and the broth.

1 tablespoon butter
1 medium onion, peeled and chopped

In a small saucepan, heat the butter and in it cook the onion until translucent.

Reserved carrots

In the container of a food processor or blender, whirl the carrots and onion until the mixture is smooth. Transfer the purée to a mixing bowl.

Reserved broth
2 cups plain yogurt
Generous grating of nutmeg
Salt
White pepper
Fine-chopped parsley

Add the broth and yogurt. Using a rotary beater, blend the soup until it is smooth. Season the soup to taste with nutmeg, salt, and pepper. Chill it for at least 4 hours. Serve it garnished with parsley.

CHILLED CUCUMBER
AND YOGURT SOUP

Yield: about 6 cups
Preparation: about 20 minutes

The soup may be prepared with many variations (see below) and you may be moved to invent some of your own.

---

3 medium-large cucumbers, peeled, halved lengthwise, and seeded	Cut one of the cucumbers into fine dice; reserve it. Into a mixing bowl, grate the remaining cucumbers.
3 scallions, chopped fine, with some of the green part *or* 1 medium-size onion, peeled and grated	To the grated cucumber, add these five ingredients. Reserve the cucumber mixture.
½ cup fine-chopped parsley	
½ teaspoon powdered cumin	
Few drops Tabasco sauce	
1 teaspoon salt	
4 cups plain yogurt Reserved cucumber mixture Reserved diced cucumber	In a mixing bowl, using a rotary beater, whip the yogurt until it is smooth. To the reserved cucumber mixture, add the yogurt. Blend well and then stir in the reserved diced cucumber. Chill the soup for at least 4 hours.

VARIATIONS: *In place of the yogurt, use 4 cupfuls of buttermilk. Or use 2 cupfuls of yogurt and 2 cupfuls of Chicken Stock or 1 cupful of stock and 1 cupful of dry white wine.*
To the completed recipe you may add one of the following:

1 cupful of diced cold cooked beef *or* chicken *or* flaked white-fleshed fish *or* chopped shrimp
2 teaspoonfuls (or more to taste) of dill weed
3 tablespoonfuls of chopped fresh mint ►

½ cupful of chopped green
onions
3 tablespoonfuls of minced red
onion
½ cupful of chopped walnuts (a
variation from Bulgaria)

CHILLED EGGPLANT
AND YOGURT SOUP*

Yield: about 6 cups
Preparation: about 1 hour

The soup may also be served hot.

---

2 medium-size or 1 very large
eggplant

With the tines of a fork, pierce the
eggplant in several places. Arrange
it on a baking sheet and cook in a
425° oven for 40 minutes. Allow it
to cool slightly; remove and discard
the skin.

In the container of a food processor
or blender, whirl the eggplant pulp
until it is smooth. Reserve the eggplant purée.

4 cups plain yogurt

In a mixing bowl, using a rotary
beater, whip the yogurt until it is
smooth.

Reserved eggplant purée
1 large clove garlic, peeled and
put through a press
Strained juice and grated
rind of 1 medium-size lemon
½ cup fine-chopped parsley
Salt
Pepper

To the yogurt, add the reserved
eggplant purée and garlic, stirring
to blend the mixture well. Stir in
the lemon juice and rind and parsley. Season the soup to taste with
salt and pepper. To serve the soup,
chill it for at least 4 hours (or heat
it over simmering water in the top
of a double boiler).

GAZPACHO
Spain

Yield: about 10 cups
Preparation: about 35 minutes

In Andalusia, where meat is scarce, gazpacho *is a cooling meal for the poor and a novel salad for the rich. Some thirty versions of the soup exist; you should therefore feel free to experiment adventurously.*

1 large cucumber, peeled, seeded, and chopped coarse
2 medium-size cloves garlic, peeled and chopped coarse
2 medium-size green peppers, seeded and chopped coarse
4 large ripe tomatoes, peeled, seeded, and chopped
3 slices stale white bread, the crusts removed, soaked in water and squeezed dry

In the container of a food processor or blender, combine these five ingredients and whirl them until the mixture is smooth.

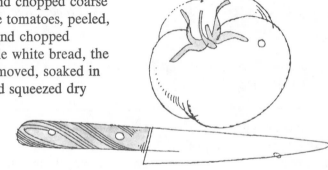

3 tablespoons red wine vinegar
6 tablespoons fine olive oil

To the contents of the container, add the vinegar and olive oil, whirling the mixture to blend it well. Transfer the mixture to a mixing bowl.

1 cup ice water

Stir in the ice water. Chill the soup for at least 4 hours.

4 cups ice water
Few drops of Tabasco sauce
Salt
Chopped toasted almonds
Garlic-flavored Croutons, page 235
Peeled, diced cucumber

Stir in the additional ice water. Season the soup to taste with Tabasco sauce and salt. Serve the *gazpacho* very cold, accompanied by as many of these garnishes as you wish, each offered separately. ▶

Chopped green pepper
Fine-chopped red onion *or*
scallions
Peeled, seeded, and chopped
tomato

VARIATION: *for* Jellied Gazpacho, *in step four soften 2½ envelopes of unflavored gelatin in ½ cupful of water or tomato juice; dissolve it over simmering water and add it to the completed soup. Chill the soup for at least 6 hours, or until it is thoroughly set.*

CHILLED LETTUCE AND PEA SOUP
United States

Yield: about 10 cups
Preparation: about 1 hour

"Fast day soup" is a recipe well known to Roman Catholic families living in New Orleans.

---

4 tablespoons butter 4 medium-size onions, peeled and chopped	In a soup kettle heat the butter and in it, over medium heat, cook the onions, covered, until translucent.
1 large head iceberg lettuce *or* 3 heads Boston lettuce, rinsed, trimmed, and shredded 1¼ pounds peas, shelled *or* 2 (10-ounce) packages frozen peas 6 cups water 4 chicken bouillon cubes 3 bay leaves 3 whole cloves 2 teaspoons sugar	To the contents of the kettle, add these seven ingredients. Bring the liquid to the boil, reduce the heat, and simmer the vegetables, covered, for 45 minutes. In the container of a food processor or blender, whirl the mixture, 2 cupfuls at a time, until it is smooth.
Salt White pepper Chopped fresh mint	Season the soup to taste with salt and pepper. Chill it for at least 4 hours. Serve it garnished with mint.

VICHYSSOISE
Chilled Cream of
Leek and Potato Soup

Yield: about 8 cups
Preparation: about 1 hour

A soup created by the late Louis Diat when he was chef of New York's Ritz-Carlton Hotel. The recipe can be made with several variations, seven of which I find especially attractive (see below).

---

4 tablespoons butter
2 small ribs celery, chopped
4 leeks, rinsed and chopped, the white part only
2 medium-size onions, peeled and chopped

In a flame-proof casserole, heat the butter and in it cook the vegetables, stirring often, until translucent.

3 medium-size potatoes, peeled and diced
4 cups Chicken or Veal Stock *or* 3 (10½-ounce) cans chicken broth

Add the potatoes and cook them, stirring, for 3 minutes. Add the stock. Bring the liquid to the boil, reduce the heat, and simmer the vegetables, covered, for 25 minutes, or until they are very tender.

In the container of a food processor or blender, whirl the mixture, 2 cupfuls at a time, until it is smooth. Transfer it to a mixing bowl.

1 cup heavy cream
Few drops of Tabasco sauce
Salt

Stir in the cream. Season the vichyssoise to taste with Tabasco sauce and salt. Chill it for at least 4 hours.

VARIATIONS: *for* Carrot Vichyssoise, *in step two in addition to the potatoes add 4 medium-size carrots, scraped and grated coarse. Complete the recipe as written.*

For Clam Vichyssoise, *in step three whirl with the potato-stock mixture 1 (6½-ounce) can of minced clams and their liquid. Complete the recipe as written.*

For Cucumber Vichyssoise, *in step three whirl with the potato-stock mixture 3 medium-size cucumbers, which have been peeled, seeded, and chopped coarse. Complete the recipe as written.* ▶

For Curried Vichyssoise, *in step one add 1½ teaspoonfuls of curry powder; in step two add 1 bay leaf to the contents of the casserole; remove it before puréeing the mixture. Complete the recipe as written.*

For Saffron-flavored Vichyssoise, *in step one add ½ teaspoonful of crumbled saffron; in step four, omit the Tabasco sauce and use in its place white pepper.*

For Sweet Potato Vichyssoise, *in step two use 2 large sweet potatoes, which have been peeled and diced, in place of the white potatoes; use Beef Stock or broth in place of chicken or veal stock. Complete the recipe as written.*

For Watercress Vichyssoise, *in step two add 1 large bunch of watercress, rinsed, dried, and chopped, the woody stems removed. Complete the recipe as written.*

YOGURT GAZPACHO

Yield: about 10 cups
Preparation: about 25 minutes

If desired, a little curry powder may be stirred into the soup.

3 cups plain yogurt
2 large cucumbers, peeled, seeded, and diced fine
2 cloves garlic, peeled and chopped fine
1 large red onion, peeled and chopped fine
1 green pepper, seeded and chopped fine
1 sweet red pepper, seeded and chopped fine (if sweet red pepper is unavailable, use 2 green peppers)
3 ripe medium-size tomatoes, peeled, seeded, and chopped
4 tablespoons wine vinegar

In a large mixing bowl, combine all of the ingredients, stirring to blend them well (there should be no "lumps" of yogurt). Refrigerate the soup for at least 4 hours and offer it in chilled cups or bowls.

2 cups tomato juice
¼ cup fine-chopped parsley
  Strained juice of 1
  medium-size lemon
1½ teaspoons salt
½ teaspoon fresh-ground
  pepper

CHILLED
YOGURT SOUP
India

Yield: about 7 cups
Preparation: about 25 minutes

Pachadi *is really a rather liquid spicy tomato salad, but is often served as an unusual cold soup.*

---

1 large onion, peeled and
  chopped fine
3 large ripe tomatoes, peeled,
  seeded, and chopped, with
  their strained juice
4 cups plain yogurt
1 teaspoon minced green chili
  pepper
½ cup (lightly packed)
  fine-chopped cilantro *or*
  fine-chopped parsley
1 teaspoon powdered cumin
1 teaspoon mustard seed,
  bruised in a mortar with
  pestle

  Salt

In a mixing bowl combine and blend all these ingredients.

Season the soup to taste with salt. Chill it for at least 4 hours.

JELLIED
BEET CONSOMMÉ

Yield: about 6 cups
Preparation: about 30 minutes
(*not including cooking the beets*)

6 medium- to large-size beets,
  scrubbed and halved
  Water

In a saucepan, arrange the beets;
over them, pour water to cover by 1
inch. Bring it to the boil, reduce the
heat, and simmer the beets, covered,
for 45 minutes, or until they are
very tender. Strain the beet liquid
and reduce it, if necessary, to 2
cupfuls. Peel, dice, and reserve the
beets and their liquid.

2 cups Beef Stock *or* 1
  (10½-ounce) can beef broth
  plus water to equal 2 cups
2 envelopes unflavored gelatin
2 cups reserved beet liquid

In a small saucepan, combine the
stock and gelatin; allow it to soften
for 5 minutes. Over medium heat,
dissolve the gelatin and add it to the
beet liquid.

  Strained juice of ½
  medium-size lemon
  Salt

Stir in the lemon juice. Adjust the
seasoning with salt. Allow the liquid to cool and then refrigerate it
until it is the consistency of heavy
syrup.

  Reserved diced beets
  Lemon slices
  Fine-chopped parsley
  Sour cream

Fold in the diced beets and chill the
consommé for at least 6 hours, or
until it is thoroughly set. Serve the
consommé garnished with lemon
slices, parsley, and sour cream.

JELLIED CONSOMMÉ
MADRILENE

Yield: about 8 cups
Preparation: about 1¼ hours

4 cups Chicken Stock *or* 3
  (10½-ounce) cans chicken
  broth
1 large carrot, scraped and
  grated coarse

In a large saucepan, combine these
ten ingredients. Bring the liquid to
the boil, reduce the heat, and simmer the mixture, covered, for 40
minutes.

1 large rib celery, chopped fine
1 large onion, peeled and chopped fine
6 sprigs parsley
1 (20-ounce) can tomatoes, with their liquid
2 bay leaves, crumbled
4 whole cloves
½ teaspoon peppercorns
2 tablespoons sugar

Strain the broth, allow it to cool, and clarify it, page 247.

Strained lemon juice
Dry sherry
Few drops of Tabasco sauce
Salt

Season the consommé to taste with lemon juice, sherry, Tabasco sauce, and salt.

2 envelopes unflavored gelatin, softened for 5 minutes in ½ cup cold water
Thin-sliced lemon
Fine-chopped parsley

In a saucepan over simmering water, dissolve the gelatin and add the consommé. Cool and chill it for at least 6 hours, or until it is thoroughly set. Serve the jellied consommé garnished with lemon slices and parsley.

JELLIED CUCUMBER SOUP
Newfoundland

Yield: about 6 cups
Preparation: about 45 minutes

6 medium-size cucumbers, peeled, seeded, and chopped
3 cups Chicken Stock *or* 2 (10½-ounce) cans chicken broth
Grated rind and strained juice of 1 medium-size lemon
¾ teaspoon ground ginger

In a saucepan, combine these ingredients. Bring the liquid to the boil, reduce the heat, and simmer the cucumber, covered, for 20 minutes.

In the container of a food processor or blender, whirl the mixture, 2 cupfuls at a time, until it is smooth.

Salt
White pepper

Season the mixture to taste with salt and pepper. ►

¼ teaspoon curry powder
1½ envelopes unflavored
gelatin, softened for 5
minutes in ⅓ cup water
Sour cream
Dill weed

Stir the curry powder into the softened gelatin and add the mixture to the contents of the processor. Whirl the soup until the gelatin is dissolved. Chill the soup for at least 6 hours, or until it is set. Garnish the soup with sour cream and dill.

VARIATION: *for* Jellied Cucumber and Chicken Soup, *in step one add 1 small onion, peeled and chopped; in step four, just before chilling the soup, add 1 cupful of diced cooked chicken meat and 2 pimientos, chopped; garnish the jellied soup with lemon wedges.*

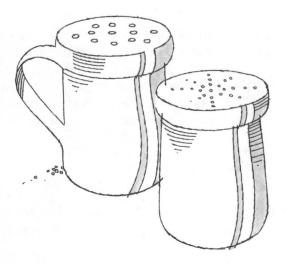

HOT CREAM AND CREAM-STYLE SOUPS

I know of no more elegant first course than a cream or cream-style soup, delicately colored, smooth on the tongue, and a delight to the palate. Like all soups, they are easily made, but unlike many soups, they are relatively economical of your time. At this point one should sing the praises of the food processor or blender, for it virtually guarantees a smooth homogeneous purée, so important in cream soups. Even with these technical marvels at my command, however, I always pour the completed soup through a strainer—just to be sure! Also—just to be sure—I use flour as a thickening much more frequently than I use egg yolk. Yes, I know, egg yolk is "classic" and does produce a richer soup; but just let the soup become a degree too hot and your efforts are lost in unattractive curdled—glop, I suppose is the word. A carefully made roux *or well-mixed* beurre manié *guarantees proper thickening and no curdling—and so I use them. You will also note that in these recipes I sometimes substitute water and bouillon cubes for stock; I do so because the essentials of cream and cream-style soups—butter, flour (eggs, sometimes potatoes), and cream (be it half-and-half, light, or heavy)— produce a dish of sufficient body to make using a rich stock optional.*

CREAM OF ALMOND SOUP

Yield: about 8 cups
Preparation: about 45 minutes

A rich and very good soup which may be made with whole or sliv-
ered almonds, blanched or lightly toasted in a 350° oven; also the
almonds may be lightly crushed, or reduced to a "flour" in the con-
tainer of a food processor or blender. My favorite way: lightly
toasted and ground in a food processor.

1 (6-ounce) package blanched almonds 1 small onion, peeled 4 cups Chicken Stock *or* 3 (10½-ounce) cans chicken broth 2 bay leaves ¼ teaspoon powdered cloves	In a large saucepan, combine these five ingredients. Bring the liquid to the boil, reduce the heat, and simmer the mixture, covered, for 30 minutes. Discard the onion and bay leaves.
3 tablespoons butter 3 tablespoons flour 1 cup milk	In a second saucepan, heat the butter and in it, over gentle heat, cook the flour for a few minutes. Gradually add the milk, stirring constantly until the mixture is thickened and smooth.
1 cup cream	To this mixture, add the almond broth, stirring until the soup is smooth. Add the cream, stirring to blend the soup well.
1 tablespoon Worcestershire sauce Salt White pepper Fine-chopped parsley	Bring the soup to serving temperature. Stir in the Worcestershire sauce. Season the soup to taste with salt and pepper. Serve it garnished with parsley.

CREAM OF ARTICHOKE SOUP*

Yield: about 6 cups
Preparation: about 30 minutes

1 (9-ounce) package frozen artichoke hearts
1 small onion, peeled and chopped coarse
1 cup Chicken Stock *or* 1 (10½-ounce) can chicken broth

In a large saucepan, combine these three ingredients. Bring the liquid to the boil, reduce the heat, and simmer the artichokes, covered, for 15 minutes, or until they are very tender.

In the container of a food processor or blender, whirl the mixture until it is smooth. Reserve the artichoke purée.

3 tablespoons butter
3 tablespoons flour
3 cups milk

In the saucepan, heat the butter and in it, over gentle heat, cook the flour for a few minutes. Gradually add the milk, stirring constantly until the mixture is thickened and smooth.

1 cup heavy cream, scalded
Reserved artichoke purée

Stir in the cream. To the milk mixture, add the artichoke purée, stirring to blend the soup well.

Salt
White pepper
Dill weed

Bring the soup to serving temperature. Season the soup to taste with salt and pepper. Serve it garnished with dill.

CREAM OF
ASPARAGUS SOUP
Denmark

Yield: about 8 cups
Preparation: about 45 minutes

The soup may be served hot or chilled.

---

1 pound fresh asparagus

Rinse the asparagus. Cut off the tips and reserve them. Cut off and discard the bottom ½ inch of the stalk. Chop the asparagus stalks medium fine and reserve them.

Reserved asparagus tips
1 cup Beef Stock *or* 1 (10½-ounce) can beef broth

Boil the asparagus tips in the stock for 10 minutes. Drain and reserve them. Reserve the liquid.

Reserved asparagus liquid
4 cups Beef Stock
Reserved chopped asparagus stalks

In a large saucepan, combine the reserved asparagus liquid and the stock. In the liquid boil the chopped asparagus stalks, covered, for 25 minutes, or until they are tender. Strain them, pressing out as much liquid as possible. Discard the residue. Return the broth to the saucepan.

2 tablespoons soft butter
2 tablespoons flour

In a small mixing bowl, combine the butter and flour and blend the mixture thoroughly. Add the *beurre manié* to the broth and bring the liquid to the boil, stirring constantly until it is thickened and smooth.

½ cup light cream, scalded
3 egg yolks

In a small mixing bowl, allow the cream to cool slightly. Add the egg yolks and beat the mixture until it is homogeneous.
To the cream, add a little of the hot soup, beating constantly. Then, away from the heat, add the cream to the contents of the saucepan, stirring constantly. ▶

1 teaspoon sugar
  Salt
  White pepper
  Reserved asparagus tips

Stir in the sugar and salt and pepper to taste. Bring the soup to serving temperature; do not allow it to boil. Serve it garnished with the asparagus tips.

VARIATION: Cream of Asparagus Soup* (*for the economically minded*); *save the raw stem ends from several servings of asparagus (perhaps three meal's worth); peel and chop them coarse. Omit steps one and two and, in step three, use Chicken Stock to cook the asparagus for 45 minutes. In step four, increase the butter and flour to 3 tablespoonfuls each. In step five use 1 cupful of heavy cream and omit the egg yolks. Complete the recipe as written, garnishing the soup with fine-chopped parsley.*

CREAM OF BEET SOUP

Yield: about 8 cups
Preparation: about 1 hour

---

6 medium-large beets *or* 2 (one-pound) cans cut beets, with their liquid

In a saucepan, boil the beets in water to cover until they are tender, about 45 minutes. Strain the beets and reserve the liquid. Peel and chop the beets and reserve them. (If using canned beets, drain them and reserve the beets and the liquid.)

3 tablespoons butter
3 tablespoons flour
Reserved beet liquid plus water to equal 4 cups

In a large saucepan, heat the butter and in it, over gentle heat, cook the flour for a few minutes. Gradually add the liquid, stirring constantly until the mixture is thickened and smooth.

1 small onion, peeled and chopped
2 bay leaves
1 teaspoon ground celery seed
½ teaspoon thyme

Add the onion and seasonings. Simmer the mixture, covered, for 20 minutes. Discard the bay leaves.

Reserved beets

In the container of a food processor or blender, purée the beets. (Add a little of the broth to facilitate this step.)

1 cup light cream, scalded
Few drops of Tabasco sauce
1 tablespoon sugar
1 teaspoon salt

To the broth, add the beet purée, cream, and seasonings. Over gentle heat, bring the soup to serving temperature.

CREAM OF
BROCCOLI SOUP*

Yield: about 8 cups
Preparation: about 50 minutes

1 medium-size carrot, scraped and chopped
1 rib celery, chopped
1 medium-size onion, peeled and chopped
1 small potato, peeled and chopped fine
2 bay leaves
4 cups Chicken Stock *or* 3 (10½-ounce) cans chicken broth

In a large saucepan, combine these six ingredients. Bring the liquid to the boil, reduce the heat, and simmer the vegetables, covered, for 25 minutes, or until the potato is very tender.

1 large head broccoli, the woody stems removed *or* 2(10-ounce) packages frozen chopped broccoli

Chop the fresh broccoli. Add the broccoli to the contents of the saucepan and boil it, covered, for 20 minutes.

In the container of a food processor or blender, whirl the mixture, 2 cupfuls at a time, until it is smooth.

1½ cups light cream, scalded
Salt
White pepper

Combine and blend the purée and cream. Bring soup to serving temperature. Season the soup to taste with salt and pepper.

VARIATION: *for those cooks who, like myself, enjoy garlic, there is* Cream of Broccoli Soup with Garlic: *sauté in 2 tablespoonfuls of butter, 2 large cloves of garlic, peeled and chopped fine; add them to the cooked broccoli before puréeing the vegetable. Complete the recipe as written.*

CREAM OF CABBAGE SOUP
United States

Yield: about 8 cups
Preparation: about 1 hour

A dish native to New York State.

---

1 small head (about 1 pound) cabbage, cored and shredded
3 medium-size onions, peeled and chopped
1 green pepper, seeded and chopped
2 slices pimiento, chopped
Bouquet garni, page 2
1 teaspoon salt
½ teaspoon pepper
Boiling water

In a soup kettle, combine the cabbage, onion, pepper, pimiento, and seasonings. Add boiling water just to cover. Simmer the vegetables, covered, for 30 minutes, or until the cabbage is very tender. Discard the *bouquet garni.*

4 cups milk
1 cup sour cream
Generous grating of nutmeg
6 slices bacon, diced, rendered, and drained on absorbent paper

In a mixing bowl, blend these three ingredients until the mixture is smooth. Stir it into the contents of the kettle; bring the soup to the simmer but do not allow it to boil.
Serve the soup garnished with the diced bacon.

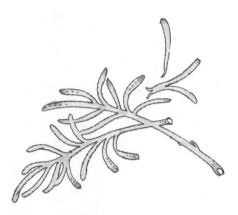

CREAM OF CARROT SOUP
France

Yield: about 8 cups
Preparation: about 1 hour

Crème nivernaise *is a classic French soup, so called because Nivernais carrots are considered especially fine.*

---

6 large carrots, scraped and grated
1 small onion, peeled and chopped
1½ teaspoons sugar
½ teaspoon salt
1½ cups water

In a large saucepan, combine these five ingredients. Bring the liquid to the boil, reduce the heat, and simmer the carrot, covered, for 20 minutes.

In the container of a food processor or blender, whirl the mixture until it is reduced to a smooth purée. Reserve it.

3 tablespoons butter
3 tablespoons flour
½ teaspoon salt
¼ teaspoon white pepper
3 cups milk

In the top of a large double boiler, heat the butter and in it, over gentle heat, cook the flour for a few minutes. Stir in the seasonings. Gradually add the milk, stirring constantly until the mixture is thickened and smooth.

Reserved carrot purée
1 cup heavy cream
Fine-chopped parsley

Into the contents of the double boiler, stir the carrot purée. Over simmering water, cook the soup, covered, for 20 minutes. Stir in the cream and bring the soup to serving temperature. Offer it garnished with chopped parsley.

VARIATION: *into the soup, before adding the cream, stir the grated rind of 1 large orange.*

FLOUR SOUP
Switzerland

Yield: about 6 cups
Preparation: about 50 minutes

Mehlsuppe, *known in Switzerland since the Middle Ages, is said to be an effective palliative against overindulgence in food and drink. It is not made with cream, but is a thickened soup having the consistency of cream soups—hence its inclusion here.*

---

4 tablespoons butter
2 medium onions, peeled and sliced thin
6 tablespoons flour

5 cups Beef Stock *or* 4 (10½-ounce) cans beef broth
Salt
Pepper
1½ cups grated natural Swiss cheese

In a large saucepan, melt the butter and in it cook the onion until translucent. Add the flour and continue to cook the mixture, stirring, until it is golden brown.

Gradually add the stock and cook the soup, stirring constantly, until it is thickened and smooth. Season it to taste with salt and pepper. Simmer the soup, covered, for 30 minutes. Into warmed bowls, spoon equal amounts of cheese. Over it, ladle the hot soup. Serve the dish at once.

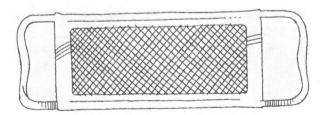

CREAM OF
CAULIFLOWER SOUP*

Yield: about 8 cups
Preparation: about 40 minutes

1 large head cauliflower, broken apart
2 cups water
3 chicken bouillon cubes
Strained juice of 1 medium lemon

In a large saucepan, combine these four ingredients. Bring the liquid to the boil and cook the cauliflower for 15 minutes, or until it is tender. Reserve the cauliflower and its liquid.

4 tablespoons butter
1 small onion, peeled and chopped
2 ribs celery, chopped

In a second saucepan, heat the butter and in it cook the onion and celery, covered, until they are tender.

4 tablespoons flour
2 cups water

Into the onion and celery, stir the flour. Over gentle heat, cook the mixture for a few minutes. Gradually add the water, stirring constantly until the mixture is thickened and smooth.

Reserved cauliflower and liquid

Combine the cauliflower, together with its liquid, and the onion mixture. In the container of a food processor or blender, whirl the mixture, 2 cupfuls at a time, until it is smooth.

2 cups light cream, scalded
2 tablespoons Madeira wine
¼ teaspoon ground nutmeg
Salt
Pepper

Stir in the cream, Madeira, and nutmeg; bring the soup to serving temperature. Season to taste with salt and pepper.

CREAM OF CELERIAC SOUP*

2 pounds celeriac (celery root), scraped and chopped
1 small onion, peeled
4 cups Chicken or Veal Stock *or* 3 (10½-ounce) cans chicken broth

In a saucepan, combine these three ingredients. Bring the liquid to the boil, reduce the heat, and simmer the celeriac for 45 minutes, or until it is very tender.

In the container of a food processor or blender, whirl the mixture, 2 cupfuls at a time, until it is reduced to a smooth purée.

½ cup heavy cream, scalded
Salt
White pepper

Into the purée, stir the cream. Bring the soup to serving temperature. Season to taste with salt and pepper.

CREAM OF CELERY SOUP

Yield: about 8 cups
Preparation: about 1 hour

6 tablespoons butter
2 medium-size carrots, scraped and chopped fine
1 large bunch celery, chopped fine
1 large onion, peeled and chopped
1 medium-size parsnip, scraped and chopped fine
1 medium-size potato, peeled and chopped fine

In a soup kettle, heat the butter and in it cook the vegetables, stirring them frequently, for 15 minutes.

4 cups Chicken or Veal Stock *or* 3 (10½-ounce) cans chicken broth

To the vegetables add the stock. Bring the liquid to the boil, reduce the heat, and simmer the vegetables, covered, for 30 minutes, or until they are very tender.

In the container of a food processor or blender, whirl the vegetables until they are reduced to a smooth purée.

1 cup heavy cream, scalded
Salt
Pepper

Stir in the cream. Bring the soup to serving temperature. Season to taste with salt and pepper.

CREAM OF
CHESTNUT SOUP*

Yield: about 7 cups
Preparation: about 25 minutes

Subtle, smooth, indecently rich, and delectable.

---

1 (15½-ounce) can
unsweetened chestnut purée
4 cups water

In a large saucepan, combine the purée and water and, using a rotary beater, blend them until the mixture is smooth.

4 chicken bouillon cubes, crushed
1 small onion, peeled and grated
3 tablespoons soft butter
1 teaspoon sugar
1 teaspoon salt
½ teaspoon white pepper

To the contents of the saucepan, add these six ingredients. Bring the mixture just to the boil, reduce the heat, and simmer it gently for 15 minutes.

1 cup heavy cream, scalded
Salt
Pepper

To the soup, add the cream, stirring to blend the mixture. Bring the soup to serving temperature. Season to taste with salt and pepper.
(The soup will not change perceptibly, but the calorie count will, if you use light cream or half-and-half, scalded, in place of heavy cream.)

CREAM OF CHICKEN
AND APPLE SOUP

Yield: about 7 cups
Preparation: about 40 minutes

An elegant first-course soup distinguished by its combination of chicken and apple flavors.

---

3 tablespoons butter
2 medium-size tart apples, peeled, cored, and chopped
1 medium-size onion, peeled and chopped

In a large saucepan, heat the butter and in it cook the apple and onion until the onion is translucent.

2 tablespoons flour
½ teaspoon salt

Add the flour and salt, stirring to blend the mixture.

3 cups Chicken Stock *or* 2 (10½-ounce) cans chicken broth plus water to equal 3 cups
¾ cup dry white wine

To the contents of the saucepan, add the stock and wine. Bring the liquid to the boil, reduce the heat, and simmer the mixture, stirring often, for 10 minutes.

Allow the mixture to cool slightly. In the container of a food processor or blender, whirl the mixture, 2 cupfuls at a time, until it is smooth. Return it to the saucepan.

1½ cups light cream
1 cup diced cooked chicken
Salt
White pepper

Stir in the cream and chicken. Bring the soup to serving temperature. Season to taste with salt and pepper.

VARIATION: *for* Curried Cream of Chicken Soup (*Senegalese Soup*), *add to the apple-onion mixture 1 tablespoonful of curry powder; in step two, increase the flour to 2½ tablespoonfuls; in step three, omit the white wine and increase the chicken stock to 5 cupfuls; in step five, use only ¾ cupful of light cream, beaten with 2 egg yolks (do not allow the soup to boil after this addition); if desired, 6 tablespoonfuls of chutney may be stirred into the completed soup. Serve the soup hot or cold, garnished with a sprinkling of chopped chives or paprika.*

CREAM OF CORN SOUP*

Yield: about 9 cups
Preparation: about 40 minutes

3 tablespoons butter
1 large onion, peeled and chopped
4 tablespoons flour

In a large saucepan or soup kettle, heat the butter and in it cook the onion until translucent. Stir in the flour and, over gentle heat, cook the mixture for a few minutes.

3 cups water
4 bouillon cubes, crushed
½ teaspoon white pepper

Gradually add the water, stirring constantly until the mixture is thickened and smooth. Stir in the bouillon powder and pepper.

3 cups fresh corn kernels, cut from the cob *or* 2 (10-ounce) packages frozen corn kernels

Add the corn kernels and simmer them, covered, for 15 minutes.

(If desired, in the container of a food processor or blender, whirl the mixture, 2 cupfuls at a time, until it is smooth.)

2 cups light cream, scalded
Worcestershire sauce (optional)
Salt
Fine-chopped parsley

Stir in the cream. Bring the soup to serving temperature. Season it to taste with Worcestershire sauce and salt. Serve it garnished with chopped parsley.

VARIATION: *for* Cream of Corn and Watercress Soup, *add, when cooking the onion, 1 bunch of watercress, rinsed, shaken dry, and chopped fine, the woody stems removed.*

For Cream of Corn and Crab Meat Soup, *add in step five 1 (7-ounce) can of crab meat, the tendons removed.*

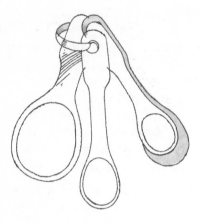

CREAM OF CRAB SOUP
United States

Yield: about 8 cups
Preparation: about 45 minutes

The traditional so-called "She-crab Soup" from South Carolina.

---

6 tablespoons butter
1½ pounds crab meat, flaked and the tendons removed

3 cups milk
3 cups light cream

Mace *or* generous grating of nutmeg
Salt
Pepper
⅓ cup cracker crumbs
3 tablespoons dry sherry

In a saucepan heat the butter and in it cook the crab meat, stirring, for 3 minutes.

In a second saucepan, combine and scald the milk and cream; add the mixture to the crab.

Season the mixture to taste with mace, salt, and pepper. Gradually add the cracker crumbs, stirring until the soup thickens; do not allow it to boil. Stir in the sherry.

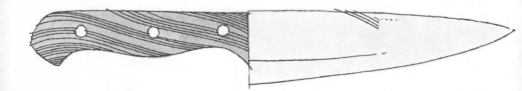

CREAM OF
CUCUMBER SOUP
Denmark

Yield: about 8 cups
Preparation: about 45 minutes

There are many cream of cucumber soups, but this one, together with its variations, is particularly good. The soup may be served hot or chilled.

---

4 tablespoons butter
4 medium-size cucumbers, peeled, seeded, and chopped
1 medium-size onion, peeled and chopped

In a large saucepan, heat the butter and in it cook the cucumbers and onion until the onion is translucent.

4 tablespoons flour

Stir in the flour and, over gentle heat, cook the mixture for a few minutes.

5 cups Chicken or Veal Stock, *or* 4 (10½-ounce) cans chicken broth
2 bay leaves
½ teaspoon white pepper

Add the stock, bay leaves, and pepper. Bring the liquid to the boil, reduce the heat, and simmer the mixture, covered, for 20 minutes. Discard the bay leaves.

In the container of a food processor or blender, whirl the mixture, 2 cupfuls at a time, until it is smooth. Return the soup to the saucepan.

1 cup heavy cream, scalded
Few drops of Tabasco sauce (optional)
Salt
1 small cucumber, sliced thin
Dill weed

Stir in the cream. Season the soup to taste with Tabasco sauce and salt. Bring the soup to serving temperature. Serve the soup garnished with a few cucumber slices and a sprinkling of dill weed.

VARIATIONS: *for Cream of Cucumber and Spinach Soup, omit step two entirely and, in step three, add 1 medium-size potato, peeled and diced, and 1 (10-ounce) package of fresh spinach, rinsed, or 1 (10-ounce) package of frozen chopped spinach, fully thawed to room temperature; complete the recipe as written.* ▶

Six chopped scallions may be substituted for the onion in step one and 2 teaspoonfuls of curry powder may be added. Three table-spoonfuls of dry sherry may be stirred into the completed soup. In place of the dill weed, garnish the soup with chopped fresh mint or a sprinkling of paprika.

CRAB, LOBSTER, OR SHRIMP BISQUE*

Yield: about 7 cups
Preparation: about 1¼ hours

I use whatever remains from serving crab, lobster, or shrimp, including the table leavings; I think you will find this recipe pleasant and less costly to make than others.

All crab, lobster, or shrimp shells remaining from having served 6 or more persons
2 cloves garlic, peeled and chopped coarse
2 medium onions, peeled and chopped coarse
2 bay leaves
4 peppercorns, crushed
½ teaspoon thyme
1 teaspoon sugar
4 cups water
4 chicken bouillon cubes

In a soup kettle, combine these nine ingredients. Bring the liquid to the boil, reduce the heat, and simmer the shells, covered, for 45 minutes.

Strain the broth through a fine sieve, making sure that all shells are emptied of liquid and any meaty parts are squeezed dry. Reserve the broth.

3 tablespoons butter
3 tablespoons flour
2 cups light cream, scalded

In a saucepan, heat the butter and in it, over gentle heat, cook the flour for a few minutes. Gradually add the cream, stirring constantly until the mixture is thickened and smooth.

Reserved broth
Salt

Stir in the reserved broth.
Correct the seasoning.

Canned crab *or* lobster *or* shrimp (optional)
Dry sherry (optional)

If desired, add crab, lobster, or shrimp (pick over crab and lobster to remove any tendons and, if you intend to freeze the soup, do not add the solids until after the bisque has come fully to room temperature). The addition of sherry, to taste, is a pleasant embellishment.

VARIATIONS: *if desired, the bisque may be given more "punch" by the addition of a little curry powder or a few drops of Tabasco sauce or about 1 tablespoonful of Worcestershire sauce. A few drops of red food coloring may be added, if you wish.*

CREAM OF EGGPLANT SOUP WITH CURRY*

Yield: about 8 cups
Preparation: about 1 hour

The soup may be served hot or chilled.

---

1 large eggplant

With the tines of a fork, pierce the eggplant in several places. On a baking sheet, cook it in a 425° oven for 40 minutes. Allow it to cool slightly. Scrape as much pulp from the skin as possible and then discard the skin.

1 medium-size potato, peeled and grated
4 cups Chicken or Veal stock, *or* 3 (10½-ounce) cans chicken broth

While the eggplant is baking, combine the potato and stock in a saucepan. Bring the liquid to the boil, reduce the heat, and simmer the potato, covered, for 25 minutes.

1 teaspoon curry powder
½ teaspoon salt
¼ teaspoon pepper

In the container of a food processor or blender, whirl the eggplant pulp until it is smooth. Add the seasonings and whirl the mixture again to blend it well. Transfer the eggplant to a saucepan.

When the potato is cooked, whirl it with its liquid, 2 cupfuls at a time, in the container of a food processor or blender until it is smooth. ▶

1 cup light cream, scalded
Few drops of Tabasco sauce
(optional)
Salt

In the saucepan, combine the egg-plant and potato mixtures. Using a rotary beater, blend them well. Add the cream, stirring. Season the soup to taste with Tabasco sauce and salt. Bring the soup to serving temperature over gentle heat or chill it for at least 4 hours.

CREAMED FISH SOUP
France

Yield: about 8 cups
Preparation: about 50 minutes

A fish soup par excellence—*a fish soup* ne plus ultra!

1 large rib celery, chopped
2 medium-size onions, peeled and quartered
4 medium-size ripe tomatoes, quartered
1 pound lean white-fleshed fish fillet
2 bay leaves
8 peppercorns
½ teaspoon thyme
1 teaspoon salt
1 cup dry white wine
3 cups Fish Stock *or* 3 cups clam juice *or* 3 cups water

In a soup kettle, combine all of these ingredients. Bring the liquid to the boil, reduce the heat, and simmer the mixture, covered, for 30 minutes. Strain it. Transfer the strained broth to a clean kettle and reserve it.

Reserved strained broth	Place the strained vegetables and fish in the container of a food processor or blender; whirl them until they are reduced to a smooth purée. Stir the purée into the broth.
1 thick slice white bread, the crust removed	In the container of a food processor or blender, combine the bread with a little of the broth; whirl them until the mixture is smooth. Add it to the contents of the kettle.
1 cup heavy cream Generous grating of nutmeg Salt White pepper Chopped chives	Bring the kettle to the boil, stir in the cream. Season the soup to taste with nutmeg, salt, and pepper. Serve the soup garnished with chopped chives.

CREAM OF GREEN ONION SOUP*

Yield: about 6 cups
Preparation: about 35 minutes

2 cups simmering water 3 bouillon cubes 2 bunches scallions, trimmed and chopped coarse, with as much of the green as is crisp	To the simmering water, add the bouillon cubes; in the broth cook the scallions, covered, for 15 minutes, or until they are very tender. In the container of a food processor or blender, whirl the mixture until it is smooth. Reserve the purée.
4 tablespoons butter 4 tablespoons flour 4 cups light cream *or* half-and-half, scalded	In a saucepan, heat the butter and in it, over gentle heat, cook the flour for a few minutes. Gradually add the cream, stirring constantly until the mixture is thickened and smooth.
Reserved scallion purée Salt White pepper Chopped parsley	Stir in the reserved purée and simmer the soup for 10 minutes, stirring occasionally. Season it to taste with salt and pepper; garnish it with parsley.

CREAM OF
GREEN PEA SOUP*

Yield: about 7 cups
Preparation: about 40 minutes

---

2 cups fresh green peas *or* 1
  (10-ounce) package frozen
  green peas
1 small onion, peeled and
  sliced
2 cups water
2 chicken bouillon cubes
1 bay leaf
¼ teaspoon white pepper

In a large saucepan, combine these six ingredients. Bring the liquid to the boil, reduce the heat, and simmer the peas, covered, for 20 minutes, or until they are very tender. Discard the bay leaf.

In the container of a food processor or blender, whirl the mixture, 2 cupfuls at a time, until it is smooth. Reserve the purée.

4 tablespoons flour
½ cup water
½ cup water
1 cup milk

In a saucepan, blend the flour and water until the mixture is smooth. To the flour mixture, add the additional water and milk. Bring the mixture to the boil, and cook it, stirring, until it is thickened and smooth.

Reserved pea purée
2 tablespoons soft butter
1 cup light cream, scalded
  Salt
  Pepper

To the flour mixture, add the reserved purée and butter. Bring the soup to the boil. Stir in the cream. Season the soup to taste with salt and pepper.

VARIATION: *for* Cream of Lima Bean Soup *use, in place of the peas, 1 (10-ounce) package frozen Lima beans. Complete the recipe as written.*

CREAM OF LETTUCE SOUP

Yield: about 8 cups
Preparation: about 40 minutes

The soup may be served hot or chilled.

---

4 tablespoons butter

1 bunch scallions, trimmed and chopped, with as much green as is crisp

1 large head lettuce (Boston, Buttercrunch), the leaves rinsed, drained, and chopped

¾ teaspoon mint

3 cups Chicken Stock *or* 2 (10½-ounce) cans chicken broth plus water to equal 3 cups

In a large saucepan, heat the butter and in it cook the scallions until they are limp.

To the scallions, add the lettuce and mint, stirring to blend the vegetables. Add the stock. Bring the liquid to the boil, reduce the heat, and simmer the lettuce, covered, for 15 minutes.

(If desired, you may whirl the lettuce mixture, 2 cupfuls at a time, in the container of a food processor or blender. This step yields a smooth soup.)

3 tablespoons cornstarch, mixed with ⅓ cup cold water

2 cups light cream, scalded

1 teaspoon sugar

2 teaspoons Worcestershire sauce

Few drops of Tabasco sauce

Salt

Pepper

Fine-chopped parsley

Green food coloring (optional)

To the lettuce mixture, add the cornstarch and light cream. Cook the soup, stirring constantly, until it is somewhat thickened and smooth.

Season the soup with the sugar and Worcestershire sauce and to taste with Tabasco sauce, salt, and pepper. Garnish with parsley. A few drops of green food coloring may be added to the finished soup.

CREAM OF FRESH MUSHROOM SOUP*

Yield: about 7 cups
Preparation: about 45 minutes

3 tablespoons butter
1 pound mushrooms, trimmed and chopped coarse
1 small onion, peeled and sliced

In a large saucepan, heat the butter and in it cook the mushrooms and onion, stirring often, until the onion is translucent.

3 tablespoons flour
3 cups water

Stir in the flour and, over gentle heat, cook the mixture for a few minutes. Gradually add the water, stirring constantly until the mixture is thickened and smooth.

2 beef bouillon cubes, crushed
½ teaspoon salt
¼ teaspoon white pepper

Add the bouillon powder and seasonings. Bring the liquid to the boil, reduce the heat, and simmer the mushroom, covered, for 20 minutes.

In the container of a food processor or blender, whirl the mixture, 2 cupfuls at a time, until it is smooth. Return the soup to the saucepan.

1 cup heavy cream, scalded
2 tablespoons dry sherry

Stir in the cream. Bring the soup to serving temperature. Just before serving, stir in the sherry.

VARIATIONS: *for a richer soup, in place of the water and bouillon cubes, use 2 cupfuls of Chicken or Veal Stock.*

For Curried Cream of Mushroom Soup, *in step one stir into the mushrooms and onion 1 teaspoonful of curry powder, or more to taste.*

For Cream of Mushroom Soup with Shrimp, *in step five stir in with the cream ½ pound of cooked shrimp, chopped coarse.*

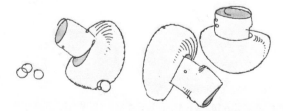

CREAM OF MUSSELS SOUP
France

Yield: about 8 cups
Preparation: about 45 minutes

Billibi *is a popular first-course soup in France.*

---

3 pounds mussels

Scrub the mussels and reserve them.

1 cup dry white wine
1 cup water
2 large onions, peeled and chopped
Bouquet garni, *page 2*

In a soup kettle, combine the wine and water; add the onion and *bouquet garni*. Bring the liquid to the boil, reduce the heat, and simmer the mixture, covered, for 10 minutes.

Reserved mussels

Add the mussels and, over high heat, steam them, tightly covered, for 10 minutes, or until they open. Discard any mussels that do not open.

Away from the heat, with a slotted spoon remove the mussels from the broth; discard the *bouquet garni*. Remove the mussels from their shells and reserve; discard the shells. Strain the broth and add just enough of it to the mussels to keep them covered. Reserve the mussels. Transfer the remaining broth to a large saucepan. Bring the broth to the simmer.

4 tablespoons soft butter
4 tablespoons flour

In a mixing bowl, combine and, using a fork, blend the butter and flour until the mixture is smooth. Add the *beurre manié* to the simmering broth, stirring constantly until it is thickened and smooth.

1 cup heavy cream, scalded
2 cups Fish Stock *or* bottled clam juice

Stir in the cream, fish stock, and saffron-water mixture. Season the soup to taste with Tabasco sauce and salt. ▶

Generous pinch of saffron,
soaked for 10 minutes in ¼
cup boiling water
Few drops of Tabasco sauce
Salt

Reserved mussels
Fine-chopped parsley

Stir in the mussels. Bring the soup to serving temperature, but do not allow it to cook (the mussels will toughen). Serve it garnished with parsley.

VARIATION: *for* Cream of Mussels Soup with Fish (*a delicious main-dish soup*), *in step six add 1½ pounds of flounder fillet, cut in bite-size pieces; simmer the fish for 10 minutes, or until it flakes easily. Complete the recipe as written.*

If desired, omit the parsley from the billibi *and use in its place 6 leaves of fresh basil, chopped fine.*

CREAM OF ONION SOUP*

Yield: about 6 cups
Preparation: about 30 minutes

5 tablespoons butter
5 large onions, peeled and chopped coarse

In a large saucepan, heat the butter and in it, over gentle heat, cook the onion, covered, for 15 minutes.

3 tablespoons flour
4 bouillon cubes, crushed

Stir in the flour and, over gentle heat, cook the mixture for a few minutes. Stir in the crushed bouillon cubes.

2½ cups milk, scalded
1 cup light *or* heavy cream, scalded
Few drops of Tabasco sauce
Salt

Gradually add the milk, stirring constantly until the soup thickens and is smooth. Blend in the cream. Season the soup to taste with Tabasco sauce and salt.

(If desired, the recipe may be puréed in the container of a food processor or blender.)

CREAM OF PARSLEY SOUP*

Yield: about 8 cups
Preparation: about 45 minutes

The soup may be served hot or chilled.

---

6 tablespoons butter

2 cups chopped parsley leaves, which have been rinsed, dried on absorbent paper, and stemmed

In a large saucepan, heat the butter and in it, over medium heat, cook the parsley, stirring often, for 5 minutes.

3 cups Chicken Stock *or* 2 (10½-ounce) cans chicken broth

1 medium-size potato, peeled and grated

1 teaspoon ground summer savory (in a mortar with a pestle)

Add the stock, potato, and summer savory. Bring the liquid to the boil, reduce the heat, and simmer the parsley, covered, for 20 minutes.

In the container of a food processor or blender, whirl the mixture, 2 cupfuls at a time, until it is smooth. Transfer it to a saucepan.

3 cups light cream
Generous grating of nutmeg
Salt
White pepper
Grated Parmesan cheese *or* fine-chopped parsley

Stir in the cream. Season the soup to taste with nutmeg, salt, and pepper. Serve the soup hot with a sprinkling of Parmesan cheese or chilled garnished with chopped parsley.

VARIATION: *for* Cream of Parsley and Tarragon Soup, *add in step one 3 tablespoonfuls of chopped fresh tarragon leaves. Complete the recipe as written.*

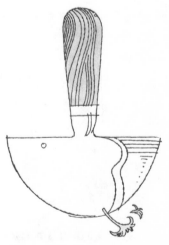

CREAM OF PARSNIP SOUP*

Yield: about 8 cups
Preparation: about 1 hour

In Old English cookery, at a time when sugar was scarce or very costly, parsnips were used as sweetening agents. This soup has a slightly sweet taste, given an edge by the onion.

---

2 pounds parsnips, scraped and chopped fine
1 medium-size onion, peeled and sliced
3 cups water
3 chicken bouillon cubes
Grating of nutmeg
¼ teaspoon pepper

In a large saucepan or soup kettle, combine these six ingredients. Bring the liquid to the boil, reduce the heat, and simmer the parsnips, covered, for 40 minutes, or until they are very tender.

In the container of a food processor or blender, whirl the mixture, 2 cupfuls at a time, until it is smooth. Return the purée to a saucepan.

2 tablespoons soft butter
2 cups light cream, scalded
Salt
Chopped parsley

To the purée, add the butter and cream, stirring to blend the soup well. Bring the soup to serving temperature. Season the soup to taste with salt.

CREAM OF
PUMPKIN SOUP*

Yield: about 8 cups
Preparation: about 45 minutes

For lazy cooks, like me—so easily made with canned pumpkin!

---

2 medium-size onions, peeled
  and grated
1 (1-pound) can pumpkin purée
4 cups Chicken Stock *or* 3
  (10½-ounce) cans chicken
  broth
1 bay leaf

In a large saucepan, combine these four ingredients. Bring the mixture to the boil, reduce the heat, and simmer it for 10 minutes. Discard the bay leaf.

1 cup light cream
  Few drops of Tabasco sauce
  Salt
  Pepper
  Fine-chopped parsley *or* fresh
  mint

Stir in the cream. Bring the soup to serving temperature. Season the soup to taste with Tabasco sauce, salt, and pepper. Garnish it with parsley or mint.

VARIATIONS: *in step one, omit the bay leaf and add ½ teaspoonful of ground ginger and 3 tablespoonfuls of cognac.*

For Pumpkin and Spinach Soup, *in step one add 1 cupful of fresh fine-chopped (packed) spinach leaves, which have been stemmed, rinsed, and dried on absorbent paper or 1 (10-ounce) package frozen chopped spinach.*

SALMON BISQUE*

Yield: about 7 cups
Preparation: about 30 minutes

Underhanded deception!—it tastes so "hard to make," but is so easy.

---

3 tablespoons butter
1 small onion, peeled and chopped fine

In a large saucepan, heat the butter and in it cook the onion until translucent.

2 tablespoons flour
4 cups milk

Stir in the flour and, over gentle heat, cook the mixture for a few minutes. Gradually add the milk, stirring constantly until the mixture is thickened and smooth; remove it from heat.

1 (1-pound) can salmon, broken up, with its liquid

In the container of a food processor or blender, whirl the salmon until it is reduced to a smooth purée. Add it to the contents of the saucepan, stirring to blend the mixture.

1 cup light *or* heavy cream, scalded
1 tablespoon Worcestershire sauce
Few drops of Tabasco sauce
Salt
2 tablespoons dry sherry
Fine-chopped parsley

Stir in the cream. Season the bisque with the Worcestershire sauce and to taste with Tabasco and salt. Stir in the sherry. Bring the soup to serving temperature. Serve it garnished with parsley.

VARIATION: *for* Scallop Bisque, *in step three omit the salmon and use in its place 1½ pounds of sea scallops, quartered. Simmer them, covered, for 10 minutes. If desired, purée the mixture in the container of a food processor or blender. Complete the recipe as written.*

SORREL SOUP
France

Yield: about 6 cups
Preparation: about 30 minutes

A variation of the classic crème Germiny. *It may be served hot or chilled.*

---

3 tablespoons butter
½ pound sorrel leaves, stemmed, rinsed, and chopped fine

In a large saucepan, heat the butter and in it cook the sorrel leaves for 15 minutes.

In the container of a food processor or blender, whirl the mixture until it is smooth. Transfer it to a saucepan.

4 cups Chicken Stock *or* 3 (10½-ounce) cans chicken broth

Add the stock, bring it to the boil, reduce the heat, and simmer the mixture, covered, for 5 minutes.

3 egg yolks
1 cup heavy cream
Salt
White pepper
Croutons, page 234

In a mixing bowl, using a rotary beater, blend the egg yolks and cream. To the mixture, add 1 cup of the simmering stock, beating. Then beat into the stock the egg-cream mixture. Do not allow the soup to boil. Season the soup to taste with salt and pepper. Serve it garnished with croutons.

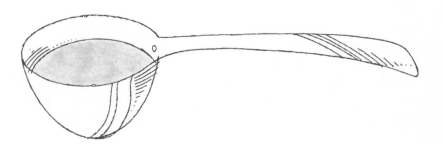

CREAM OF SPINACH SOUP*

Yield: about 8 cups
Preparation: about 30 minutes

The soup may be served hot or chilled.

4 tablespoons butter 1 small onion, peeled and grated	In a large saucepan, heat the butter and in it cook the onion for a few minutes.
4 tablespoons flour 6 cups water 6 chicken bouillon cubes, crushed	Stir in the flour and, over gentle heat, cook the mixture for 3 minutes. Gradually add the water, stirring constantly until the mixture is thickened and smooth. Stir in the crushed bouillon cubes.
1 (10-ounce) package fresh spinach, rinsed, *or* 1 (10-ounce) package frozen chopped spinach, fully thawed to room temperature	Add the spinach, bring the mixture to the boil, and cook the vegetable, covered, for 10 minutes.
	In the container of a food processor or blender, whirl the mixture, 2 cupfuls at a time, until it is smooth. Transfer it to a saucepan.
1 cup heavy cream 1 tablespoon Worcestershire sauce Few drops of Tabasco sauce Salt	Stir in the cream. Season the soup to taste with the Worcestershire and Tabasco sauces and salt. Bring the soup to serving temperature or chill it for at least 4 hours.

VARIATIONS: *for* Cream of Spinach Soup (*Italy*), *in place of the water and bouillon cubes, use 6 cupfuls of Veal Stock; in step five, reduce the cream to ½ cupful, into which you have beaten 3 egg yolks; into this mixture, beat 1 cupful of the simmering broth before stirring it, away from the heat, into the contents of the saucepan; omit the Worcestershire and Tabasco sauces, and season the soup to taste with grated nutmeg, salt, and white pepper; garnish it with a sprinkling of grated Parmesan cheese. Do not allow the soup to boil.*

For Cream of Spinach Soup (*Norway*), *in place of the water and bouillon cubes, use 6 cupfuls of Beef Stock or 4 (10½-ounce) cans of beef broth plus water to equal 6 cupfuls. Complete the recipe as written. Serve the soup over Cheese Toasts, page 234.*

For Cream of Spinach and Basil Soup, *in step three add 1 (loosely packed) cupful of fresh basil leaves, which have been stemmed, rinsed, and shaken dry. Complete the recipe as written.*

For Cream of Spinach and Clam Soup, *in step three add 2 (6½-ounce) cans of minced clams, with their liquid. Complete the recipe as written.*

For Cream of Spinach and Mushroom Soup, *in step four add to the purée ½ pound of mushrooms trimmed and chopped fine; simmer the mixture for 5 minutes, stirring often. Complete the recipe as written.*

For Cream of Spinach and Scallion Soup, *in step five add 6 scallions, trimmed, sliced thin, and cooked until limp in 2 tablespoonfuls of butter. Complete the recipe as written.*

For Cream of Spinach and Sorrel Soup, *in step three add 1 (packed) cupful of fresh sorrel leaves, which have been stemmed, rinsed, and shaken dry. Complete the recipe as written.*

For Cream of Spinach and Watercress Soup, *in step three add 1 (packed) coarse-chopped cupful of watercress, which has been rinsed and drained, the woody stems removed.*

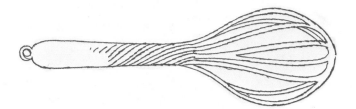

FRESH TOMATO SOUP*

Yield: about 12 cups
Preparation: about 1 hour

The soup may be served hot or chilled.

---

4 medium-size carrots, scraped and chopped
6 ribs celery, chopped, with their leaves
1 large onion, peeled and chopped
1 bunch parsley, rinsed
3 pounds ripe tomatoes, quartered
4 bay leaves
Handful of fresh basil leaves
3 sprigs marjoram
6 sprigs mint
3 sprigs thyme

In a soup kettle, combine these ten ingredients and, over medium heat, cook them, covered, for 40 minutes, or until the carrots are very tender. (The tomatoes will make adequate liquid.)

Into a large saucepan, strain the mixture, forcing through the sieve as much pulp as possible.

6 tablespoons soft butter
6 tablespoons flour

In a small mixing bowl, combine the butter and flour. With a fork, blend the mixture until it is smooth. To the contents of the saucepan, add the *beurre manié*. Over medium heat, stir the mixture constantly until it is thickened and smooth.

2 cups light cream, scalded
1 cup heavy cream, scalded
2 cups milk, scalded

Stir in the cream and milk.

1 tablespoon sugar
Salt
White pepper

Season the soup to taste with the sugar and salt and pepper.

Garlic-flavored Croutons, page 235 *or* fine-chopped fresh mint

Serve the soup hot garnished with croutons or chilled garnished with mint.

TUNA BISQUE*

Yield: about 6 cups
Preparation: about 45 minutes

The soup may be served hot or chilled.

---

3 tablespoons butter
1 small carrot, scraped and grated
1 clove garlic, peeled and chopped
1 medium-size onion, peeled and chopped

In a saucepan, heat the butter and in it cook the carrot, garlic, and onion until the onion is translucent.

1 large ripe tomato, peeled, seeded, and chopped

Stir in the tomato and simmer the mixture for 3 minutes.

2 cups water
1 cup dry white wine
4 chicken bouillon cubes
1½ tablespoons raw natural rice

To the contents of the saucepan, add the water, wine, bouillon cubes, and rice. Bring the liquid to the boil, reduce the heat, and simmer the rice, covered, for 25 minutes, or until it is very tender.

In the container of a food processor or blender, whirl the mixture, 2 cupfuls at a time, until it is smooth. Transfer it to a second, larger saucepan.

1 (7-ounce) can water-pack tuna, with its liquid

In the container of a food processor or blender, whirl the tuna until it is reduced to a smooth purée. Add it to the contents of the saucepan and blend the mixture well.

1 cup heavy cream
2 teaspoons Worcestershire sauce
Salt
White pepper
Thin-sliced scallions

Stir in the cream. Season the soup with Worcestershire sauce and to taste with salt and pepper. Bring the soup to serving temperature or chill it for at least 4 hours. Serve it garnished with scallions.

VARIATION: *for* Curried Tuna Bisque, *in step one add 1 to 1½ teaspoonfuls of curry powder.*

✳   **HOT CREAM AND CREAM-STYLE SOUPS 187**   ✳

CREAM OF TURNIP SOUP*

Yield: about 6 cups
Preparation: about 50 minutes

---

4 medium-size white turnips, scraped and chopped
4 cups water
4 beef bouillon cubes

In a large saucepan, combine these three ingredients. Bring the liquid to the boil, reduce the heat, and simmer the turnips, covered, for 30 minutes, or until they are very tender.

In the container of a food processor or blender, whirl the mixture, 2 cupfuls at a time, until it is smooth. Reserve the purée.

4 tablespoons butter
4 tablespoons flour

In a saucepan, heat the butter and in it, over gentle heat, cook the flour for a few minutes.

½ teaspoon powdered cumin
Reserved turnip purée

Stir in the cumin. Gradually add the turnip purée, stirring constantly, until the mixture is thickened and smooth.

1 cup heavy cream, scalded
Salt

Stir in the cream. Season the soup to taste with salt.

VARIATION: *for a less rich soup, use light cream or milk.*

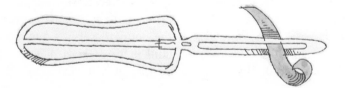

CREAM OF FRESH VEGETABLE SOUP*

Yield: about 10 cups
Preparation: about 45 minutes

½ pound green beans, trimmed, rinsed, and cut in ½-inch pieces

4 medium-size carrots, scraped and sliced thin

1 small cauliflower, trimmed and separated into flowerets

¾ cup green peas

3 new potatoes, peeled and diced

6 radishes, trimmed and sliced thin

4 chicken bouillon cubes, crushed

½ teaspoon white pepper
Water

In a soup kettle, combine these nine ingredients, adding cold water barely to cover. Bring the liquid to the boil and cook the vegetables over high heat, uncovered, for 15 minutes, or until they are tender. Strain them through a colander, reserving the broth and vegetables.

3 tablespoons butter
3 tablespoons flour

In the soup kettle, heat the butter and in it, over gentle heat, cook the flour for a few minutes.

Reserved broth

Gradually add the reserved broth, stirring constantly until the mixture is thickened and smooth. ▶

1 cup light cream or milk,
  scalded
  Reserved vegetables
2 cups rinsed, stemmed,
  chopped fresh spinach leaves
  Salt
  Pepper
  Dill weed

Stir in the cream or milk. Add the vegetables and spinach; simmer the soup for 5 minutes. Season it to taste with salt and pepper. Serve it garnished with dill.

CREAM OF VEGETABLE SOUP
France

Yield: about 10 cups
Preparation: about 1 hour

Potage crème Saint-Germain *is traditionally made with* crème fraiche; *the substitution of heavy cream works nicely.*

---

4 tablespoons butter
1 medium-size carrot, scraped
  and chopped fine
1 large rib celery, chopped
  fine
1 medium-size onion, peeled
  and chopped fine
1 small white turnip, scraped
  and chopped fine

In a flame-proof casserole, heat the butter and in it cook the vegetables until the onion is translucent.

1 cup drained canned white
  kidney beans
1 teaspoon sugar
5 cups Veal or Chicken Stock
  or 4 (10½-ounce) cans
  chicken broth

To the contents of the casserole, add these three ingredients. Bring the liquid to the boil, reduce the heat, and simmer the mixture, covered, for 30 minutes.

In the container of a food processor or blender, whirl the mixture, 2 cupfuls at a time, until it is smooth. Transfer it to a large saucepan.

1½ cups diced cooked mixed fresh vegetables *or* 1 (10-ounce) package frozen mixed vegetables, cooked until just tender according to the directions on the package
1 cup heavy cream
 Salt
 White pepper
 Fine-chopped parsley *or*
 Croutons, page 234

Stir in the mixed vegetables and cream. Bring the soup to serving temperature and season it to taste with salt and pepper. Serve it garnished with parsley or croutons.

CREAM OF WATERCRESS SOUP*

Yield: about 6 cups
Preparation: about 25 minutes

The soup may be served hot or chilled.

3 tablespoons butter
1 medium-size onion, peeled and chopped

In a saucepan, heat the butter and in it cook the onion until translucent.

3 tablespoons flour
4 chicken bouillon cubes, crushed

Stir in the flour and, over gentle heat, cook the mixture for a few minutes. Stir in the crushed bouillon cubes.

3 cups water

Gradually add the water, stirring constantly until the mixture is thickened and smooth.

1 large bunch watercress, rinsed, shaken dry, and chopped coarse

Add the watercress and simmer it, covered, for 10 minutes.

In the container of a food processor or blender, whirl the mixture, 2 cupfuls at a time, until it is smooth. Transfer it to a saucepan. ►

2 cups light cream
Few drops of Tabasco sauce
Salt
Paprika

Stir in the cream. Bring the soup to serving temperature or chill it for at least 4 hours. Season it to taste with Tabasco sauce and salt. Serve it garnished with paprika.

VARIATIONS: *for* Curried Cream of Watercress Soup, *in step one add 1 teaspoonful of curry powder to the cooking onion. Complete the recipe as written.*

For Cream of Watercress Soup with Shrimp, *in step six with the cream add ½ pound of shrimp, cooked, shelled, deveined, and chopped fine or 1 (6½-ounce) can of shrimp, drained and chopped fine.*

For Cream of Watercress Soup with Tarragon, *in step one add 1 tablespoonful of chopped fresh tarragon leaves to the cooking onion. Complete the recipe as written.*

For Chilled Watercress and Yogurt Soup, *make the recipe as written using, in step six, 2 cupfuls of plain yogurt in place of the cream; blend the soup well to eliminate any yogurt lumps. Chill the soup for at least 4 hours.*

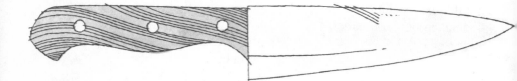

CREAM OF ZUCCHINI SOUP*

Yield: about 8 cups
Preparation: about 30 minutes

The soup may be served hot or chilled.

---

3 tablespoons butter
1 small clove garlic, peeled and chopped
1 small onion, peeled and chopped

In a large saucepan, heat the butter and in it cook the garlic and onion until translucent.

3 tablespoons flour

Stir in the flour and, over gentle heat, cook the mixture for a few minutes.

4 large zucchini, trimmed and chopped

Add the zucchini and, over gentle heat, cook the mixture, stirring, for 10 minutes.

3 cups hot water
3 chicken bouillon cubes, crushed

Add the water and crushed bouillon cubes. Bring the mixture to the boil, reduce the heat, and simmer the zucchini, covered, for 15 minutes, or until it is very tender.

In the container of a food processor or blender, whirl the mixture, 2 cupfuls at a time, until it is smooth. Transfer it to a saucepan.

2 cups light cream
Salt
White pepper
Fine-chopped parsley

Stir in the cream. Bring the soup to serving temperature or chill it for at least 4 hours. Season it to taste with salt and pepper. Serve it garnished with parsley.

VARIATIONS: *for* Cream of Zucchini and Clam Soup, *in step five add 1 (6½-ounce) can of minced clams with their liquid; in step six, use 1 cupful of light and 1 cupful of heavy cream.*

For Curried Cream of Zucchini Soup, *in step one add 1 teaspoonful of curry powder to the cooking onion.*

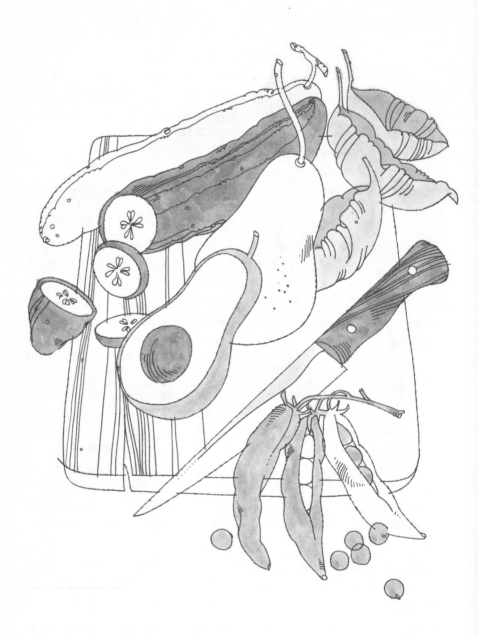

CHILLED CREAM AND CREAM-STYLE SOUPS

Cream and cream-style soups, always festive dishes with which to begin a meal, are especially attractive served chilled, particularly in warm weather. There is no last-minute heating to contend with.

Although the soups in this section are designed to be served chilled, there is nothing to prevent your serving them hot if you so desire.

CHILLED CREAM OF AVOCADO SOUP*

Yield: about 8 cups
Preparation: about 20 minutes

3 large ripe avocados, peeled, seeded, and chopped coarse
3 cups Chicken Stock *or* 2 (10½-ounce) cans chicken broth plus water to equal 3 cups
1½ cups light cream

In the container of a food processor or blender, combine these three ingredients and whirl them until the mixture is smooth. Transfer it to a mixing bowl.

Strained lemon juice
Worcestershire sauce
Few drops of Tabasco sauce
Salt

Season the soup to taste with the lemon juice, the Worcestershire and Tabasco sauces, and salt. Chill it for at least 4 hours.

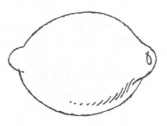

CHILLED CREAM OF BASIL SOUP*

Yield: about 8 cups
Preparation: about 45 minutes

Because basil is one of my favorite herbs, I could not resist using it as the basis for a chilled summer soup.

---

3 tablespoons butter
6 scallions, trimmed and chopped, with as much of the green as is crisp

In a large saucepan or soup kettle, heat the butter and in it cook the scallions until they are limp.

4 tablespoons flour
4 cups water

Stir in the flour and, over gentle heat, cook it for a few minutes. Gradually add the water, stirring constantly until the mixture is thickened and smooth.

3 cups rinsed, stemmed (packed) fresh basil leaves
4 chicken bouillon cubes
2 bay leaves

To the contents of the saucepan, add the basil leaves, bouillon cubes, and bay leaves. Simmer the mixture, covered, for 30 minutes.

In the container of a food processor or blender, whirl the mixture, 2 cupfuls at a time, until it is smooth. Transfer it to a mixing bowl.

1 cup light cream, scalded
Salt
Pepper

Stir in the cream and adjust the seasoning to taste. Chill the soup for at least 4 hours.

CHILLED CREAM OF CARROT SOUP

Yield: about 6 cups
Preparation: about 40 minutes

6 large carrots, well scrubbed (it is not necessary to scrape them) and cut in ½-inch rounds

1 bunch scallions, trimmed and chopped, the white part only; reserve as much of the green as is crisp

2½ cups Chicken Stock *or* 2 (10½-ounce) cans chicken broth

In a saucepan, combine these three ingredients. Bring the liquid to the boil, reduce the heat, and simmer the vegetables, covered, for 30 minutes, or until the carrots are very tender.

In the container of a food processor or blender, whirl the mixture, 2 cupfuls at a time, until it is smooth. Transfer the mixture to a mixing bowl.

1 cup sour cream
Few drops of Tabasco sauce
Salt
Reserved green scallions, chopped fine

Using a rotary beater, blend the sour cream with the purée. Season the soup to taste with Tabasco sauce and salt. Chill the soup for at least 4 hours. Serve the soup garnished with reserved green scallions.

CHILLED CREAM OF CUCUMBER AND TOMATO SOUP*

Yield: about 8 cups
Preparation: about 40 minutes

1 pound ripe tomatoes, quartered
3 tablespoons butter

In a large saucepan, combine the tomatoes and butter. Cook the tomatoes, covered, stirring them often, for 20 minutes.

4 cups water
4 bouillon cubes, crushed

To the tomatoes, add the water and bouillon cubes. Bring the liquid to the boil and, over high heat, cook the mixture for 5 minutes. Strain it into a mixing bowl.

2 large cucumbers, peeled, seeded, and chopped coarse

In the container of a food processor or blender, whirl the cucumber until it is reduced to a smooth purée. Stir it into the tomato mixture.

½ cup sour cream
1 tablespoon tomato paste
Few drops of Tabasco sauce
Salt
1 medium-size cucumber, peeled, seeded, and diced

Blend in the sour cream and tomato paste. Add the Tabasco sauce and adjust the seasoning to taste. Chill the soup for at least 4 hours. Serve the soup garnished with diced cucumber.

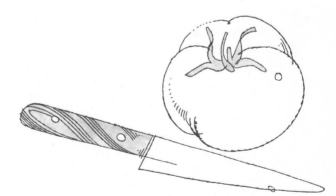

CHILLED
LENTIL SOUP*

Yield: about 10 cups
Preparation: about 2 hours

---

3 tablespoons butter *or* fine olive oil
1 large clove garlic, peeled and chopped coarse
2 large onions, peeled and sliced

In a soup kettle, heat the butter and in it cook the garlic and onion, covered, until they are limp.

8 cups water
8 chicken bouillon cubes
2 cups lentils
2 bay leaves
1½ teaspoons basil
1 (6-ounce) can tomato paste
2 teaspoons sugar
½ teaspoon pepper

To the contents of the kettle, add these eight ingredients. Bring the liquid to the boil, reduce the heat, and simmer the lentils, covered (stir them occasionally), for 1½ hours, or until they are very tender. Discard the bay leaves.

In the container of a food processor or blender, whirl the mixture, 2 cupfuls at a time, until it is smooth. Transfer to a mixing bowl.

Cool and then chill the purée for at least 4 hours. When chilled, it will be thick.

Light cream *or* milk
Salt
Fine-chopped scallions, the white part only

To complete the soup, use a rotary beater to blend in as much light cream or milk as is necessary to bring the mixture to the consistency you prefer. Season the soup to taste with salt. Garnish each serving with chopped scallions.

CHILLED CREAM OF PEA SOUP

Yield: about 5 cups
Preparation: about 20 minutes

It could not be easier—or more refreshing—for a warm evening's supper.

---

1 (10-ounce) package frozen tiny peas, fully thawed to room temperature
2 cups milk
1 teaspoon sugar
¾ teaspoon salt
¼ teaspoon white pepper

In the container of a food processor or blender, combine these five ingredients and whirl them until the mixture is smooth. Transfer it to a mixing bowl.

1 cup light cream
Garlic salt
Fine-chopped fresh mint

Stir in the cream. Season the soup to taste with garlic salt. Chill it for at least 4 hours. Serve it garnished with mint.

VARIATION: *add 6 medium-size mint leaves, their stems removed, to the ingredients in step one. When serving the soup, garnish it with dill weed instead of mint.*

CHILLED SORREL SOUP
Israel

Yield: about 10 cups
Preparation: about 40 minutes

Schav, a classic of Jewish cookery, is easily made—and very good.

---

2 medium-size onions, peeled and chopped fine
1 pound *schav* (sorrel or sour grass), stemmed, rinsed, and shredded
2 teaspoons salt
8 cups water

In a large saucepan, combine these four ingredients. Bring the liquid to the boil, reduce the heat, and simmer the mixture, covered, for 25 minutes.

1 tablespoon strained fresh lemon juice
Sugar (optional)

Season the soup to taste with the lemon juice and sugar.

2 eggs, beaten
Sour cream

Away from the heat, gradually whip the eggs into the soup. Allow the soup to cool and then chill it for at least 4 hours. Serve it garnished with sour cream.

CHILLED CREAM OF SPLIT PEA SOUP WITH MINT*

Yield: about 12 cups
Preparation: about 2 hours

2 cups green split peas
8 cups water
8 bouillon cubes

In a soup kettle, combine these three ingredients. Bring the liquid to the boil, reduce the heat, and simmer the peas, covered, for 45 minutes.

1 clove garlic, peeled and chopped
2 large onions, peeled and chopped
2 bay leaves
1 teaspoon celery seed
¼ teaspoon ground cloves
1 cup (tightly packed) fresh mint leaves *or* 3 tablespoons dried mint leaves

To the simmering peas, add these six ingredients and continue to cook the mixture, covered, for 45 minutes longer. Stir the mixture occasionally to prevent its sticking to the pan. Remove and discard the bay leaves.

In the container of a food processor or blender, whirl the mixture, 2 cupfuls at a time, until it is smooth. Transfer the purée to a mixing bowl.

2 cups light cream *or* half-and-half, scalded
Salt
White pepper
Chopped fresh mint

Into the purée, stir the cream. Season the soup to taste with salt and pepper.
Allow the soup to cool and then chill it for at least 4 hours.
When the soup is chilled, it will have thickened; if necessary, add a little milk, stirring, until it reaches the consistency you prefer. Serve the soup garnished with mint.

CHILLED CREAM OF TOMATO SOUP WITH CURRY*

Yield: about 10 cups
Preparation: about 1 hour

4 tablespoons butter
1 bunch scallions, trimmed and chopped coarse, with as much of the green as is crisp

In a large saucepan or soup kettle, heat the butter and in it cook the scallions until they are wilted.

1 medium-large potato, peeled and chopped
1½ teaspoons curry powder

Add the potato and curry powder, stirring to blend the vegetables well.

2 pounds ripe tomatoes, the stem ends removed, chopped coarse
5 allspice berries, crushed
Several fresh basil leaves *or* 1 teaspoon dried basil
2 bay leaves
4 cups water
4 bouillon cubes

To the contents of the saucepan, add the tomatoes and seasonings.
Add the water and bouillon cubes. Bring the liquid to the boil, reduce the heat, and simmer the vegetables, covered, for 30 minutes. Strain the mixture into a mixing bowl. Discard the residue.

1 cup heavy cream, scalded
Salt
Pepper
Fine-chopped fresh mint

Stir in the cream. Season the soup to taste with salt and pepper. Chill it for at least 4 hours. Serve it garnished with mint.

CHILLED CREAM OF WATERCRESS SOUP*

Yield: about 6 cups
Preparation: about 45 minutes

3 tablespoons butter 1 small onion, peeled and chopped fine 1 large bunch watercress, stemmed, rinsed, and chopped fine	In a large saucepan, heat the butter and in it cook the onion and watercress, stirring, until the onion is translucent.
3 cups Chicken Stock *or* 2 (10½-ounce) cans chicken broth plus water to equal 3 cups	Add the stock, bring the liquid to the boil, reduce the heat, and simmer the watercress, covered, for 20 minutes.
1 (3-ounce) package cream cheese, at room temperature and cut in small pieces	Add the cream cheese, stirring until it is melted.
3 tablespoons cornstarch mixed with ½ cup cold milk 1½ cups milk	To the contents of the saucepan add the cornstarch mixture and the milk, stirring constantly until the soup is thickened and smooth.
1 tablespoon Worcestershire sauce Few drops of Tabasco sauce Salt	Add the Worcestershire sauce and season to taste with Tabasco and salt. Chill the soup for at least 4 hours.

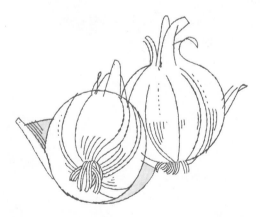

CHEESE SOUPS

Cheese soups are undeniably rich fare; not only have they the usual soup ingredients but they also have the added richness and flavor of cheese. They require a bit more care in preparation, for the cheese should be melted gently and should not be overcooked; overcooking tends to change its flavor.

CHEDDAR SOUP
England

Yield: about 6 cups
Preparation: about 45 minutes

1 large carrot, scraped and sliced thin
1 medium-size rib celery, chopped fine
1 large onion, peeled and chopped fine
1 cup boiling water

In a large saucepan, combine the vegetables and boiling water; cook them, covered, for 20 minutes, or until they are tender. Reserve them and their liquid. (If a smooth soup is desired, allow the mixture to cool and then whirl it, 2 cupfuls at a time, in the container of a food processor or blender.)

3 tablespoons butter
3 tablespoons flour
2½ cups milk

In a second saucepan, heat the butter and, over gentle heat, cook the flour for a few minutes. Gradually add the milk, stirring constantly until the mixture is thickened and smooth.

Reserved vegetables and their liquid
1½ cups Chicken Stock *or* 1 (10½-ounce) can chicken broth
1¼ cups sharp Cheddar cheese, grated coarse
Worcestershire sauce
Salt
Pepper

To the mixture, add the vegetables and their liquid, the stock, and the cheese. Away from the heat, stir the mixture to melt the cheese. Season the soup to taste with Worcestershire sauce, salt, and pepper.

VARIATION: *for a hearty main-dish soup, in step one add 2 cupfuls of diced potato and, in step three, 1 cupful of diced cooked ham.*

CHEESE SOUP
Austria

Yield: about 8 cups
Preparation: about 45 minutes

In Vienna, the soup would be made with a Gervais-type cheese; our cream cheese makes an excellent substitute.

6 tablespoons butter
3 medium-size ribs celery, chopped fine
6 scallions, the white part only, trimmed and chopped fine

In a large saucepan, heat the butter and in it cook the celery and scallions, covered, for 15 minutes.

In the container of a food processor or blender, whirl the vegetables until they are reduced to a smooth purée. Return the purée to the saucepan.

6 tablespoons flour
1½ teaspoons salt
4 cups Chicken or Veal Stock *or* 3 (10½-ounce) cans chicken broth

Into the purée, stir the flour and, over gentle heat, cook the mixture for a few minutes. Stir in the salt. Gradually add the stock, stirring constantly until the mixture is thickened and smooth.

2 (8-ounce) packages cream cheese at room temperature
2 cups plain yogurt at room temperature
Chopped chives

To the contents of the saucepan, add first the cream cheese, stirring until it is melted, and then the yogurt, stirring until the soup is well blended. Serve it garnished with chopped chives.

CHEESE SOUP
Switzerland

Yield: about 8 cups
Preparation: about 50 minutes

6 slices bacon, diced	In a large saucepan, render the bacon until crisp, drain it on absorbent paper, and reserve it. Discard all but 3 tablespoons of the fat.
8 scallions, trimmed and chopped, with as much green as is crisp 1 medium-size rib celery, chopped fine	In the remaining fat, cook the scallions and celery until they are limp.
½ cup quick-cooking rolled oats 5 cups Chicken Stock *or* 4 (10½-ounce) cans chicken broth 1 teaspoon salt ¼ teaspoon white pepper	Add these four ingredients, stirring to blend the mixture well. Bring the liquid to the boil, reduce the heat, and simmer uncovered for 30 minutes.
	Allow it to cool somewhat. In the container of a food processor or blender, whirl the mixture, two cupfuls at a time, until it is smooth. Return the mixture to a large saucepan.
½ cup Appenzeller *or* Emmenthaler cheese, grated ½ cup Gruyère cheese, grated	Bring the soup to serving temperature. Remove it from the heat and add the grated cheeses, stirring constantly until they are melted.
¼ cup heavy cream ¼ cup dry white wine 4 teaspoons dill weed Reserved bacon	Over gentle heat, stir in the cream, wine, and dill. Serve the soup garnished with the bacon.

CHEESE AND CORN CHOWDER
Netherlands

Yield: about 8 cups
Preparation: about 35 minutes

---

2 cups water
1 large potato, peeled and diced
2 bay leaves
½ teaspoon cumin seed
½ teaspoon sage
1 teaspoon salt

In a soup kettle, bring the water to the boil. Add the potato and seasonings. Cook the potato, covered, for 10 minutes, or until it is tender. Reserve the mixture.

3 tablespoons butter
1 medium onion, peeled and chopped
3 tablespoons flour
1½ cups heavy cream

In a saucepan, melt the butter and in it cook the onion until translucent. Stir in the flour and, over gentle heat, cook it for a few minutes. Gradually add the cream, stirring constantly until the mixture is thickened and smooth. Reserve it.

1½ cups fresh corn cut from the cob *or* 1 (10-ounce) package frozen corn kernels, fully thawed to room temperature
3 tablespoons chopped chives
⅓ cup parsley, chopped fine
Grating of nutmeg
Salt
Pepper

To the potato mixture, add the corn. Stir in the cream mixture. Stir in the chives and parsley. Add the seasonings to taste and then simmer the soup, covered, for 10 minutes.

1½ cups Edam or Gouda cheese, grated
1 cup dry white wine

Over gentle heat, add the cheese, stirring constantly until it is melted. Stir in the white wine.

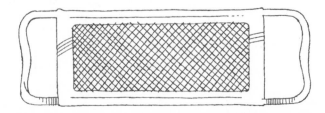

CHILLED CHEESE AND CUCUMBER SOUP
Netherlands

Yield: about 7 cups
Preparation: about 25 minutes

2 tablespoons butter
2 tablespoons flour
5 cups milk

In a saucepan, melt the butter and in it, over gentle heat, cook the flour for a few minutes. Gradually add the milk, stirring constantly until the mixture is thickened and smooth.

1½ cups Edam or Gouda cheese, grated
Salt
White pepper

Remove the saucepan from the heat and add the cheese, stirring until it is melted. Add the seasonings to taste.

1 large cucumber, peeled, seeded, and grated

Stir in the cucumber. Chill the soup for at least 4 hours.

Parsley, chopped fine

Serve it garnished with parsley.

CHEESE AND LEEK SOUP
Switzerland

Yield: about 8 cups
Preparation: about 45 minutes

6 leeks, rinsed and sliced, with the tender green part
⅓ cup raw natural rice
6 cups Beef Stock *or* 4 (10½-ounce) cans beef broth plus water to equal 6 cups
Salt
Pepper

In a large saucepan, combine the leek, rice, and stock. Bring the liquid to the boil, reduce the heat, and simmer the leek for 20 minutes, or until it and the rice are tender. Season the broth to taste with salt and pepper.

1½ cups Swiss cheese, grated
1½ cups dry white wine

In the top of a double boiler over simmering water, combine the cheese and wine. Melt the cheese, stirring until it is smooth. Into heated dishes, spoon equal amounts of the cheese. Over it, ladle the boiling soup and serve.

ONION SOUP
England

Yield: about 8 cups
Preparation: about 45 minutes

3 tablespoons butter
3 medium ribs celery, chopped
3 large onions, peeled and chopped
3 tablespoons flour

In a large saucepan, melt the butter and in it cook the celery and onion until translucent. Stir in the flour and cook the mixture for a few minutes.

Generous grating of nutmeg
1 teaspoon salt
½ teaspoon white pepper
3 cups milk
1½ cups Chicken Stock *or* 1 (10½-ounce) can chicken broth

Stir in the seasonings. Gradually add the milk and stock, stirring constantly until the mixture is thickened and smooth. Over gentle heat, simmer the soup, covered, for 10 minutes.

1½ cups mild Cheddar cheese, grated

Remove the soup from the heat and add half of the cheese, stirring until it is melted. Serve the soup, offering the remaining cheese separately.

CHEESE AND ONION SOUP*

Yield: about 8 cups
Preparation: about 30 minutes

3 tablespoons butter
1 large Spanish ("Bermuda") onion, peeled and chopped

In a large saucepan, heat the butter and in it cook the onion until translucent.

3 tablespoons flour
3 bouillon cubes, crushed
½ teaspoon white pepper

Stir in the flour and cook the mixture over gentle heat for a few minutes. Stir in the bouillon powder and pepper.

2 cups water
3 cups milk
2 cups grated Cheddar cheese (sharp or mild—the choice is yours)

Gradually add the water, stirring constantly until the mixture is thickened and smooth. Add the milk and then the cheese, stirring until the cheese is melted.

CHEESE AND ONION SOUP
France

Yield: about 10 cups
Preparation: about 45 minutes

5 tablespoons butter 5 large yellow onions, peeled and chopped	In a large saucepan, melt the butter and in it cook the onion until translucent. In the container of a food processor or blender, purée the mixture. Return the purée to the saucepan.
3 cups Chicken Stock *or* 2 (10½-ounce) cans chicken broth plus water to equal 3 cups	Add the stock and simmer the mixture, covered, for 30 minutes.
5 cups milk, scalded	Remove the saucepan from the heat and gradually stir in the milk.
3 egg yolks, beaten	Slowly beat ½ cup of the hot broth into the egg yolk; then beat the yolk-broth mixture back into the contents of the saucepan.
	Over gentle heat, cook the soup, stirring constantly, until it thickens slightly (do not allow it to boil). Remove it from the heat.
⅓ cup heavy cream ¾ cup grated Gruyère cheese Nutmeg	Add the cream and cheese, stirring to melt the cheese. Serve the soup garnished with a grating of nutmeg.

CREAM OF TOMATO SOUP WITH CHEESE

Yield: about 8 cups
Preparation: about 45 minutes

4 tablespoons butter 2 medium onions, peeled and chopped fine 2 tablespoons flour ¾ teaspoon salt ½ teaspoon white pepper 2 cups milk	In a large saucepan, melt the butter and in it cook the onion until translucent. Add the flour and, over gentle heat, cook the mixture, stirring, for a few minutes. Stir in the seasonings. Gradually add the milk, stirring constantly until the mixture is thickened and smooth.

1 (1-pound) can tomatoes, sieved
1 cup Chicken Stock *or* 1 (10½-ounce) can chicken broth

Stir in the tomatoes and stock. Bring the soup to the boil, reduce the heat, and simmer it, covered, for 15 minutes.

½ cup heavy cream, scalded
1 cup sharp Cheddar cheese, grated

Away from the heat, stir in the hot cream and cheese.

VEGETABLE SOUP WITH GOUDA CHEESE
Netherlands

Yield: about 10 cups
Preparation: about 45 minutes

6 tablespoons butter
3 medium carrots, scraped and diced fine
1 small cauliflower, cut in flowerets
6 medium onions, peeled and sliced
3 medium potatoes, peeled and diced fine

In a soup kettle, melt the butter and in it cook the vegetables, stirring, for 8 minutes.

5 cups Chicken Stock *or* 4 (10½-ounce) cans chicken broth

Add the broth, bring the liquid to the boil, reduce the heat, and simmer the vegetables, covered, for 20 minutes, or until they are just tender.

3 slices bacon
6 slices bread

Render the bacon until crisp; remove it and drain on absorbent paper. Discard all but 3 tablespoons of the fat. In the remaining fat, toast the bread slices on each side until golden.

6 (⅛-inch) slices Gouda cheese

On a baking sheet, arrange the toasted bread; on each slice, arrange half a strip of bacon and a slice of cheese. Melt the cheese under a hot broiler (about 3 minutes). ▶

½ cup grated Gouda cheese

To serve the soup, arrange a piece of the toast in individual warmed dishes. Ladle the soup over the toasts. Garnish each serving with a sprinkling of the grated cheese.

WINTER SQUASH SOUP WITH CHEESE*

Yield: about 9 cups
Preparation: about 1 hour

The soup may be made with 2 (10-ounce) packages of frozen Hubbard squash.

⅓ cup yellow corn meal
2 medium-size onions, peeled and chopped fine
1 pound winter squash of your choice, peeled and diced
5 cups water
4 bouillon cubes
4 teaspoons sugar

In a large saucepan or soup kettle, combine these six ingredients. Bring the liquid to the boil, reduce the heat, and simmer the squash, covered, for 40 minutes or until it is tender.

(If desired, you may whirl the mixture, 2 cupfuls at a time, in the container of a food processor or blender.)

Salt
Pepper
1 cup grated Cheddar cheese (mild or sharp, the choice is yours)

Season the soup to taste with salt and pepper. Just before serving, stir the cheese into the hot soup.

HOT AND COLD
FRUIT AND NUT SOUPS

Fruit soups are popular in the Scandinavian and Slavic countries; they are rarities, or at least curiosities, to the majority of soup-eaters in this part of the world. Here, then, is a fine field of exploration for the soup-maker—new tastes, new textures, even new uses for soup, for fruit soups may be successfully served as dessert.

CHILLED ALMOND SOUP
WITH GRAPES
Spain

Yield: about 6 cups
Preparation: about 25 minutes

The recipe is improved by being made 24 hours in advance of serving.

---

1 (6-ounce) package blanched slivered almonds
1 large clove garlic, peeled and coarsely chopped
¾ teaspoon powdered cumin
1 teaspoon salt

In the container of a food processor or blender, whirl the almonds until they are reduced to the consistency of bread crumbs. Add the garlic, cumin, and salt and continue to whirl the mixture for a few seconds.

½ cup fine olive oil
⅓ cup white wine vinegar
1 cup ice water

With the motor running, add, in order, the olive oil, vinegar, and ice water. Transfer the mixture to a bowl.

3 cups ice water

Add the additional ice water, stirring the soup to blend it well. Chill it for at least 4 hours. Before serving it, smooth the consistency with a rotary beater.

1 medium-size bunch seedless grapes, stemmed, rinsed, and dried on absorbent paper

If desired, you may halve the grapes lengthwise (I think the soup is improved by doing so). Garnish the soup with the grapes.

ALMOND
AND RAISIN SOUP
Mexico

Yield: about 7 cups
Preparation: about 35 minutes

---

4 tablespoons butter
1 cup blanched slivered almonds
1 cup golden seedless raisins

In a large saucepan, heat the butter and in it, over medium heat, cook the almonds and raisins for 10 minutes; stir them often.

2 medium-size onions, peeled and chopped fine

Add the onion and cook it until translucent (more butter may be added as necessary). ▶

| 3 large ripe tomatoes, peeled and seeded | Transfer the contents of the sauce-pan and the tomatoes to the container of a food processor or blender. Whirl them until the mixture is smooth. |
| 3 cups Beef Stock *or* 2 (10½-ounce) cans beef broth plus water to equal 3 cups
Salt
Pepper | Return the purée to the saucepan, add the beef stock, and simmer the soup for 10 minutes. Season it to taste with salt and pepper. |

APPLE SOUP
Russia

Yield: about 9 cups
Preparation: about 45 minutes

An admirable soup, smooth, redolent of apple, and given a pleasant "edge" by the wine.

4 large tart apples, peeled and cored (reserve the peelings and cores) 2 cups Chicken or Veal Stock *or* 1 (10½-ounce) can chicken broth plus water to equal 2 cups 1 medium-size onion, peeled and chopped coarse 2 bay leaves	In a large saucepan, combine these four ingredients. Bring the liquid to the boil, reduce the heat, and simmer the fruit, covered, for 20 minutes, or until it is very soft. Remove the bay leaves.
	In the container of a food processor or blender, whirl the mixture, 2 cupfuls at a time, until it is smooth. Return it to the saucepan.
½ cup sugar 3 tablespoons flour	Sift together the sugar and flour and add the mixture to the contents of the saucepan. Bring the mixture just to the boil, stirring constantly until it is thickened and smooth. Reserve the purée.
Reserved peelings and cores 1 cup water 1 bay leaf	In a saucepan, combine these three ingredients. Bring the liquid to the boil, reduce the heat, and simmer the mixture for 15 minutes. Strain the mixture. Discard the residue.

Reserved apple purée
1 cup sour cream *or* yogurt

2 cups dry red wine
Strained juice of 1 small
lemon

Combine the strained liquid and apple purée. Using a rotary beater, blend in the sour cream or yogurt.

Stir in the wine and lemon juice. Over gentle heat, bring the soup to serving temperature; do not allow it to boil.

APPLE AND
PUMPKIN SOUP
United States

Yield: about 8 cups
Preparation: about 30 minutes

Nothing could be more American than apples and pumpkins, which unite happily in this soup, transformed, if desired, into a main-course dish by the addition of Cheddar cheese.

---

4 tablespoons butter
3 tart apples, peeled and
   grated
2 cups canned pumpkin purée
2 tablespoons sugar
¼ teaspoon ground nutmeg
1½ teaspoons salt
¼ teaspoon white pepper

In a large saucepan, melt the butter. To it, add the apple, pumpkin purée, and seasonings. Over gentle heat, cook the mixture, stirring often, for 10 minutes.

1¼ cups Chicken Stock *or* 1
   (10½-ounce) can chicken
   broth
3 cups milk, scalded

Gradually add the broth and then the milk, stirring constantly. Simmer the soup, covered, for 5 minutes. ▶

1 cup grated mild Cheddar cheese (optional)

Remove the soup from the heat and add the cheese, stirring constantly until it is melted. Serve the soup at once.

VARIATION: *in step one omit the pumpkin; in step two, cook 2 medium-size yams, which have been peeled and diced, in the stock and milk for 20 minutes, or until tender; in the container of a food processor or blender, whirl the mixture, 2 cupfuls at a time, until it is smooth. Complete the recipe as written.*

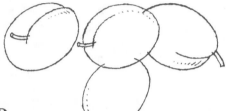

CHILLED APRICOT SOUP
Norway

Yield: about 8 cups
Preparation: about 55 minutes

The soup may also be served hot.

---

1 (11-ounce) package dried pitted apricots
6 cups water

In a large saucepan, combine the apricots and water; allow the fruit to soak for 1 hour.

⅓ cup sugar (or more to taste)
Pinch of salt

Add the sugar and salt. Cook the apricots, covered, for 35 minutes, or until they are very tender.

In the container of a food processor or blender, whirl the apricots, 2 cupfuls at a time, until the mixture is smooth. Return the purée to the saucepan.

¼ cup quick-cooking tapioca, softened in ½ cup water
Strained juice of ½ medium-size lemon
Sour cream

Into the purée, stir the tapioca. Over gentle heat, bring the soup to the boil, stirring until it thickens. Stir in the lemon juice. Allow the soup to cool and then chill it for at least 4 hours. Serve it garnished with sour cream.

AVOCADO SOUP
Mexico

Yield: about 7 cups
Preparation: about 30 minutes

---

2 tablespoons butter
1 medium-size onion, peeled and chopped fine

In a large saucepan, heat the butter and in it cook the onion until translucent.

2 tablespoons flour

Stir in the flour and, over gentle heat, cook the mixture for a few minutes.

1 large ripe tomato, peeled, seeded, and chopped
4 cups Beef Stock *or* 3 (10½-ounce) cans beef broth
Salt
Pepper

Stir in the tomato. Gradually add the stock, stirring constantly until the mixture is thickened and smooth. Season the mixture to taste with salt and pepper. Remove the saucepan from the heat.

3 large ripe avocados, peeled, seeded, and chopped coarse
½ cup light cream

In the container of a food processor or blender, whirl the avocado and cream until the mixture is smooth.

Thin-sliced scallions (the white part only)

Add it to the contents of the saucepan, stirring to blend the soup well. Bring the soup to serving temperature. Serve it garnished with a sprinkling of scallions.

CHILLED BLUEBERRY SOUP
Norway

Yield: about 6 cups
Preparation: about 25 minutes

1 envelope unflavored gelatin, softened for 5 minutes in ¼ cup cold water
4 cups strained fresh-squeezed orange juice
3 tablespoons sugar
Pinch of salt

Over simmering water, dissolve the gelatin. In a mixing bowl combine the gelatin, orange juice, sugar, and salt, stirring to dissolve the sugar. Chill the mixture until it is syrupy.

1 pint blueberries, picked over, rinsed, and drained
Fine-chopped fresh mint
Lemon wedges *or* sour cream (optional)

Into the gelatin, stir the blueberries. Chill the soup for at least 4 hours. Serve the soup garnished with a sprinkling of mint and, if desired, lemon wedges or sour cream.

CHERRY SOUP

Yield: about 6 cups
Preparation: about 25 minutes

The soup may be served hot or chilled.

2 (1-pound) cans water-pack pitted sour red cherries, with their liquid
1 cup strained fresh orange juice
Grated rind of 1 medium-size orange
4 teaspoons cornstarch
½ teaspoon cinnamon
⅓ cup sugar (or more to taste)
Pinch of salt

In the container of a food processor or blender, combine these seven ingredients and whirl them until the mixture is smooth. Transfer it to a large saucepan.

1 cup dry red wine
Sour cream

Into the contents of the saucepan, stir the wine. Cook the soup, stirring constantly, until it comes just to the boil and thickens. Serve the soup garnished with sour cream.

VARIATION: *for* Danish Cherry Soup, *in step one, add the grated rind and strained juice of 1 medium-size lemon; reserve the drained cherries from one can and stir them into the completed recipe; bring the soup to serving temperature and instead of the sour cream, garnish the soup with Sweet Croutons, page 235.*

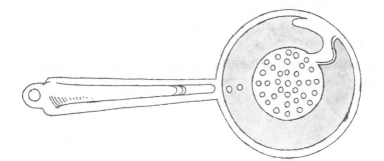

CHILLED CREAM OF CHERRY SOUP
Hungary

Yield: about 8 cups
Preparation: about 40 minutes

---

1 (1-pound) can pitted sour cherries, with their liquid
1 (1-pound) can pitted sweet cherries, with their liquid
1 (3-inch) piece cinnamon stick
3 cups water

In a saucepan, combine these four ingredients. Bring the mixture to the boil, reduce the heat, and simmer it, covered, for 15 minutes. Discard the cinnamon stick.

Sugar
Salt

Season to taste with sugar and salt.

4 tablespoons flour
½ cup water

Blend the flour and water until the mixture is smooth. Add it to the contents of the saucepan and cook the mixture, stirring constantly until it is thickened and smooth. Allow it to cool and then chill it for 4 hours.

1 cup heavy cream, chilled
1 cup dry red wine, chilled

Stir in the cream and wine at the time of serving.

VARIATION: *for a smooth soup, purée the mixture in the container of a food processor or blender after seasoning it with salt and sugar.*

CRANBERRY SOUP*

Yield: about 8 cups
Preparation: about 45 minutes

For a smoother soup, whirl the cranberry mixture, 2 cupfuls at a time, in the container of a food processor or blender, after seasoning it with salt and pepper.

---

1 (1-pound) package fresh cranberries, rinsed and picked over
4½ cups water
3 chicken bouillon cubes
1 small onion, peeled and chopped fine
2 bay leaves

In a large saucepan or soup kettle, combine these five ingredients. Bring the liquid to the boil, reduce the heat, and simmer the cranberries, covered, for 30 minutes, or until they are very tender.

¾ cup sugar (or more to taste)
Salt
Pepper

Into the contents of the saucepan, stir the sugar. The soup should be tart-sweet; add more sugar if necessary. Season the soup to taste with salt and pepper.

Strained juice and grated rind of 1 small lemon
3 tablespoons cornstarch, mixed with ½ cup water

Stir in the juice and lemon rind. Add the cornstarch, stirring the soup constantly until it is thickened and smooth.

Sour cream

Serve the soup hot, garnished with sour cream.

DRIED FRUIT SOUP
Middle East

Yield: about 10 cups
Preparation: about 2 hours

The beets add color, the curry powder gives a pungent flavor.

---

1 pound lean stewing lamb
2 large beets, scraped and grated
1 large onion, peeled and sliced
6 cups boiling water

In a large saucepan, combine these four ingredients. Return the water to the boil, skimming it if necessary.

1 cup lentils
2 teaspoons curry powder
1 teaspoon salt

1 (11-ounce) package mixed
  dried fruits, the pits removed
  from the prunes

Strained fresh lemon juice
Fine-chopped fresh mint

Add the lentils and seasonings. When the water returns to the boil, reduce the heat, and simmer the mixture, covered, for 1 hour, or until the lentils are tender.

To the contents of the saucepan, add the mixed fruits. Continue to simmer the soup, covered, for 30 minutes.

Remove and dice the lamb; return it to the saucepan. Season the soup to taste with lemon juice (it should have a pleasant tang) and offer it garnished with chopped mint.

DRIED FRUIT SOUP
Sweden

Yield: about 10 cups
Preparation: about 2 hours

The Swedish classic—a welcome dessert soup.
The soup may be served hot or chilled.

½ cup coarse-chopped dried
  apples
½ cup chopped dried apricots
¼ cup currants
½ cup coarse-chopped dried
  peaches
18 pitted prunes
⅓ cup golden raisins
 2 (3-inch) pieces cinnamon
  stick
 6 whole cloves
 6 cups cold water

In a large saucepan, combine these nine ingredients. Bring the liquid to the boil, reduce the heat, and simmer the fruit, covered, for 1 hour.

 1 medium-size lemon, sliced
  very thin and seeded
¼ cup quick-cooking tapioca
⅓ cup sugar (or more to taste)
  Pinch of salt
  Water, if needed
  Sour cream

Add the lemon slices, tapioca, and seasonings; add water, if needed. Continue to simmer the soup, uncovered, stirring it often, for 20 minutes, or until the tapioca dissolves. When serving the soup, offer the sour cream separately.

PLUM SOUP
Germany

Yield: about 10 cups
Preparation: about 45 minutes

The soup may be served hot or chilled.

1½ pounds purple plums, pitted
Zest of 1 medium-size lemon
Zest of 1 medium-size orange
2 (3-inch) pieces cinnamon stick
¼ cup sugar
8 cups water

In a large saucepan, combine these six ingredients. Bring the liquid to the boil, reduce the heat, and simmer the plums, covered, for 30 minutes, or until they are soft. Discard the lemon and orange zests and cinnamon sticks.

(If desired, the plums may be puréed in the container of a food processor or blender.)

5 tablespoons cornstarch mixed with ⅓ cup water
⅓ cup dry white wine
Salt
Sour cream

To the simmering soup, add the cornstarch and water, stirring until the soup is thickened and smooth. Stir in the wine. Season the soup to taste with salt. Serve it garnished with sour cream.

VARIATION: *in step one use 1 (1-pound-14-ounce) can of purple plums, drained and pitted; reserve the liquid. To the liquid add Beef Stock or beef broth or water to equal 4½ cupfuls. In a mixing bowl, combine the purée (you use step two), the liquid, and 1 cup of sour cream; using a rotary beater, blend the mixture. Omit the cornstarch, water, and wine. Season the soup to taste with ground cinnamon and salt. Chill it for at least 4 hours. Garnish it with Sweet Croutons, page 235.*

PRUNE SOUP
United States

Yield: about 10 cups
Preparation: about 40 minutes

A recipe from Pennsylvania Dutch country.

---

1 (11-ounce) package tenderized pitted prunes, halved
7 cups water

In a large saucepan, combine the prunes and water. Cook the prunes, covered, for 15 minutes, or until they are tender.

2 cups raisins	Add the raisins and continue to cook the fruit for 10 minutes.
½ cup flour ½ cup milk	Blend the flour and milk until the mixture is smooth. Add it to the contents of the saucepan, stirring constantly until the soup is thickened.
Sugar Salt Milk (optional)	Season the soup to taste with sugar and salt. Thin the soup, if desired, with additional milk.

STRAWBERRY SOUP
Russia

Yield: about 8 cups
Preparation: about 30 minutes

Although usually served hot, I find the soup equally good offered chilled as a first course in summer.

1 quart strawberries, hulled, rinsed, and drained 1 cup sour cream 1 cup dry white wine ½ cup sugar Pinch of salt	In the container of a food processor or blender, whirl these five ingredients until the mixture is smooth. Transfer the mixture to a large saucepan.
4 cups cold water Sugar, if desired	To the purée, add the water and, using a rotary beater, blend the mixture well. Adjust the seasoning to taste with additional sugar. Over gentle heat, bring the soup to serving temperature; do not allow it to boil.

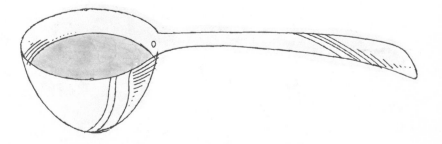

GARNISHES

I must admit at the outset that I am not partial to additives, foreign objects, often unidentified, swimming about in my soup. If the dish is well made, I feel it should be allowed to speak for itself. To give a soup visual appeal, nothing is more successful than a sprinkling of fine-chopped parsley.

Despite my prejudice against many garnishes, there are occasions (and soups) which are enhanced by them. One case in point is (or are) dumplings, light and tender, which transform a homely soup into a satisfying one-dish meal. The same may be said of meatballs. Hot tomato-based soups and many vegetable soups (including, of course, minestrone) *are dishes fit for the gods when a dollop of* pesto genovese *has been added to them. Similarly, most fish soups are improved by a spoonful of* rouille.

Quick and Easy Garnishes

The following garnishes are fairly standard, require only minimal preparation, and are generally prepared from items at hand.

For Thick Soups
Crisp diced bacon
Grated cheese
Croutons
Fine-chopped fresh herbs

For Legume Soups
Crisp diced bacon
Croutons
Frankfurters, cut in ¼-inch
    rounds and heated in the soup
Fine-chopped fresh herbs
Paper-thin lemon slices
Fine-chopped onion

**For Hot or Chilled
Cream and Cream-style Soups**
Crisp diced bacon
Grated cheese
Croutons
Fine-chopped fresh herbs
Grated lemon rind
Chopped nuts
Paprika

**For Hot Soups
and Clear Soups**
Avocado slices
Dumplings
Fine-chopped fresh herbs
Paper-thin slices of lemon, lime,
    or orange

Julienne of cooked meats or
    vegetables
Cooked thin pasta

**For Chilled Thin
Soups**
Avocado slices
Thin-sliced cucumber
Fine-chopped fresh herbs
Paper-thin slices of lemon, lime,
    or orange
Fine-chopped scallions
Sour cream
Thin-sliced tomato

For Jellied Soups
Caviar (black lumpfish roe or red
    salmon roe)
Fine-chopped fresh herbs
Paper-thin slices or wedges of
    lemon, lime, or orange

**Suggested
Fresh Herbs for Garnish**
Basil
Chives
Marjoram
Parsley
Summer savory
Tarragon
Watercress

Prepared Garnishes

CREPES CELESTINES
France

Yield: about 18 crepes
Preparation: about 1 hour

For clear soups. The crepes may be individually packaged in plastic wrap and kept for long periods in the freezer.

5 tablespoons melted butter
2 eggs
1½ cups flour
2 cups hot milk
2 tablespoons fine-chopped parsley (optional)
½ teaspoon salt

Soft butter

In the container of a blender, combine these ingredients and, on medium speed, whirl them until the mixture is completely blended and smooth.

Allow the batter to stand for at least 2 hours before making the crepes.

Heat a 5- or 6-inch crepe pan or skillet; butter it lightly. Pour in only sufficient batter to cover the bottom of the pan (about 3 table-spoonfuls); tilt the pan to spread the batter evenly. Cook the crepe until the surface is almost dry and the edges curl. Turn the crepe with a spatula or your finger tips and brown the other side. Remove the crepe from the pan onto paper toweling. Make the rest of the crepes the same way.

Roll up the crepes and cut them in ⅛-inch rounds. Add the rounds to the soup, in which they will unwind as thin strips.

One-half crepe per serving makes an adequate garnish.

EGGS MIMOSA

Yield: about 6 servings

A light and pretty garnish for clear and cream soups which could not be easier to prepare: force through a sieve 3 hard-cooked eggs and sprinkle some over the surface of each bowl of soup. Voilà! If you want to be fancier, halve the eggs lengthwise, remove the yolk and reserve the white; force the yolk through a sieve and with it fill the cavity of the reserved whites; sprinkle the yolk with a little fine-chopped parsley or paprika, and float the whites on the surface of the soup.

CROUTONS

Croutons are only as good as the bread from which they are made; use a top quality bread at least two days old.
Allow 1 slice of bread per serving. Cut the crust from the bread. You may now proceed in one of two ways:
1) *Cut the bread in ½-inch cubes. Over medium heat, melt butter in a skillet, add the bread cubes, and fry them, stirring them often, until they are golden.*
2) *Butter the bread slices and then cut them in ½-inch cubes. Arrange them on a baking sheet and toast them in a preheated 350° oven for about 10 minutes, or until they are golden.*

Olive oil may be substituted for butter.

For Cheese Croutons, *prepare plain croutons as directed above and, while they are still hot, toss them with a blend of: 1 teaspoonful of paprika and ½ cupful of grated Parmesan cheese.*

Related to croutons are Cheese Toasts, *which may be floated on the surface of clear soups or served separately. To make them, combine 4 tablespoonfuls of soft butter with 4 tablespoonfuls of grated Parmesan or other strong-flavored cheese; with this mixture, spread thin-sliced bread, the crusts removed; cut the bread to the size you desire; bake the toasts in a preheated 450° oven for 10 minutes, or until they are golden.*

For Garlic-flavored Croutons, *blend the butter* or *oil with 1 clove of garlic, peeled and put through a press.*

For Sweet Croutons (*to accompany fruit soups*), *prepare plain croutons as directed above and, while they are still hot, toss them with superfine granulated sugar; in a colander, shake off any excess sugar.*

DUMPLINGS

There is only one inviolate rule in cooking dumplings: once the dough has been added to the simmering soup and the utensil covered, do not *remove the cover during the prescribed cooking time. Transgression of this rule will in all probability yield a fallen, leaden dumpling. Apart from this consideration, however, dumplings and their recipes can and should serve as a point of departure for your culinary imagination.*

PLAIN BAKING-POWDER DUMPLINGS

Yield: 6 large or 12 small dumplings
Preparation: about 30 minutes

1 cup flour
2 teaspoons baking powder
½ teaspoon sugar
½ teaspoon salt

In a mixing bowl, combine and blend these four ingredients.

½ cup milk

Add the milk and, using a fork, stir the mixture until the flour is just moistened.

Onto the surface of the simmering soup, spoon the dumpling dough in individual portions. Cook the dumplings, covered, for 20 minutes. Serve the dumplings at once. ►

VARIATIONS: *for* Rich Baking-powder Dumplings, *in step two reduce the milk to ⅓ cupful; add to it 1 egg and 2 tablespoonfuls of melted butter or vegetable oil; with a rotary beater, blend the mixture well. Complete the recipe as written.*

For Herb Dumplings, *use the recipe for either Plain or Rich Dumplings and add in step one 1 tablespoonful of fine-chopped fresh basil or parsley or tarragon or ½ to ¾ teaspoonful of a dried herb of your choice.*

BREAD DUMPLINGS

Yield: 6 to 8 dumplings
Preparation: about 20 minutes

3 cups ½-inch bread cubes, cut from old bread ½ teaspoon baking powder ¼ cup flour ¾ teaspoon salt ¼ teaspoon pepper	In a mixing bowl, combine and blend these five ingredients.
½ cup milk 1 egg 1 tablespoon melted butter *or* vegetable oil 1 tablespoon fine-chopped parsley A grating or two of onion	In another mixing bowl, combine and, using a rotary beater, blend thoroughly these five ingredients.

Using a fork, stir the liquid into the dry ingredients until the mixture has the consistency of a light but lumpy dough.

Onto the surface of the simmering soup, spoon the dough in individual portions. Cook the dumplings, covered, for 8 minutes. Serve them at once.

LIVER DUMPLINGS
Germany

Yield: 6 dumplings
Preparation: about 30 minutes

Leberknödel are a popular soup garnish in German-speaking countries.

½ pound beef liver, all connective tissue and veins removed	In the container of a food processor or blender, reduce the liver to a smooth purée.
3 stale Vienna rolls Water	Soak the rolls in water for 5 minutes. Squeeze them dry and break them up.
1 egg, beaten ½ teaspoon marjoram ½ teaspoon salt Pinch of pepper	In a mixing bowl, combine the liver, rolls, egg, and seasonings. Using a fork or knife, cut the mixture until it is well blended.
	Onto the simmering surface of the soup, drop the mixture in individual portions. Cook the dumplings, covered, for 15 minutes. Serve them at once.

HAM DUMPLINGS

Yield: 6 to 8 dumplings
Preparation: about 45 minutes

An attractive addition to split pea and other legume soups made with a ham bone.

---

1 cup ground lean cooked ham ¾ cup flour 1 teaspoon baking powder Pinch of mace ½ teaspoon powdered sage ½ teaspoon thyme ½ teaspoon salt	In a mixing bowl, combine and blend these seven ingredients.
1 egg ⅓ cup milk	In another mixing bowl, using a rotary beater, blend the egg and milk. Using a fork, stir the liquid into the dry ingredients until they are just moistened. ►

Onto the surface of the simmering soup, spoon the dumpling dough in individual portions. Cook the dumplings, covered, for 15 minutes. Serve them at once.

MATZO BALLS

Yield: 6–12 matzo balls
Preparation: about 40 minutes

A homely delight of Jewish cookery. It is important to refrigerate the dough for 2 hours before cooking it.

⅓ cup chicken fat
2 eggs
1 cup matzo meal
1 teaspoon salt

In a mixing bowl, combine these ingredients. Using a fork, blend them well.

⅓ cup water

Gradually add the water, beating constantly, until the batter is stiff. Refrigerate the batter for 2 hours.

Boiling salted water *or* Chicken Stock

With your hands, moistened in cold water, quickly mold walnut-size balls of the dough. Drop them into boiling water to cover. Cook them, covered, for 30 minutes. Drain them.
Serve the matzo balls in clear soup.

WON TON DUMPLINGS
China

Yield: about 18 dumplings
Preparation: about 50 minutes

1½ cups flour
1 teaspoon salt

Into a mixing bowl, sift the flour and salt.

1 egg
3 tablespoons water

In a second bowl, combine the egg and water; beat the mixture with a fork.

Add the egg to the flour, blending the mixture until it yields a stiff dough (more water may be added if necessary). On a floured surface, knead the dough until it is smooth. Cover it with a damp cloth and allow it to stand for 30 minutes.

Cornstarch

On a surface rubbed with cornstarch, roll the dough very thin. Cut it in 2½-inch squares.

In the center of half of the squares, arrange 1 teaspoonful of filling (see below). Cover the filling with a second square of dough, moisten the edges with water, and crimp the dumpling tightly closed with the tines of a fork. Allow the *won ton* to dry for several hours.

Into the simmering soup, drop the dumplings. Cook them, covered, for 10 minutes.

Meat or Shrimp Filling: *mix together ½ pound of fine-ground beef, chicken, pork, or cooked shrimp with 6 fine-chopped water chestnuts and 2 tablespoonfuls of bamboo shoots, 3 scallions, 2 tablespoonfuls of ginger root, all chopped as fine as possible before measuring; season the mixture with 1 teaspoonful of salt and a grating of pepper.*

Vegetable filling: *in a skillet, in 2 tablespoonfuls of butter cook 1 cupful of chopped parsley leaves, and 1 rib of celery, 1 small onion, and ½ seeded green pepper, all chopped fine; when the vegetables are wilted, add 1 slice of bread, which has been soaked in water and squeezed dry; blend the mixture well and season it to taste with a little ground ginger and salt and pepper.*

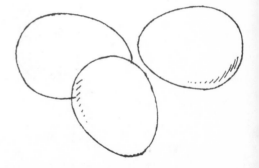

MEATBALLS
Netherlands

Yield: 6 meatballs
Preparation: about 20 minutes

½ pound ground lean beef
2 slices stale bread, the crusts removed, soaked in a little milk, and squeezed dry
1 egg, beaten
Generous grating of nutmeg
½ teaspoon salt
⅛ teaspoon pepper

In a mixing bowl, combine and blend well all of the ingredients. Refrigerate the mixture for 1 hour.

Shape the mixture into small balls about 1 inch in diameter. Cook them, covered, on the surface of the simmering soup for 10 minutes.

VARIATIONS: *add 1 small onion, peeled and grated; in place of the bread slices, use ¼ cupful of bread crumbs; in place of the nutmeg, use an herb of your choice.*

In a skillet, heat 2 tablespoonfuls of butter and in it brown the meatballs; drain on absorbent paper and add them to the completed soup.

For Cheese-flavored Meatballs, *omit the nutmeg and add 3 tablespoonfuls of grated Parmesan cheese.*

The meatballs may also be made of chicken, pork, or veal; if made of pork, it is recommended that they be thoroughly browned before being added to the soup. See also pages 27, 28, and 29.

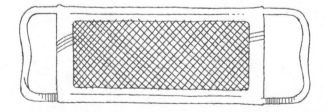

PESTO GENOVESE
Italy

Yield: about 1½ cups
Preparation: about 15 minutes

A superb sauce from Genoa, known to most of us as an accompaniment to pasta dishes. Pesto genovese, which is often made in a mortar with a pestle, is also an admirable garnish for such dishes as minestrone *and legume soups. It refrigerates and freezes well.*

---

2 large cloves garlic, peeled
½ cup olive oil
2 tablespoons water

In the container of a food processor or blender, whirl these three ingredients for 15 seconds.

2 tablespoons pine nuts (*pignoli*)

Add the pine nuts and whirl the mixture for 15 seconds longer.

1 cup (packed) fresh basil leaves, which have been stemmed, rinsed, and shaken dry
2 tablespoons soft butter
4 tablespoons grated Parmesan cheese
Pinch of salt

With the motor running, add the basil leaves, a few at a time, until they are reduced to a smooth purée. Add the butter, cheese, and salt. Whirl the mixture until it is homogeneous.

Transfer the sauce to a small bowl and press plastic wrap onto its surface (exposed to air, it will darken). Refrigerate it.

To serve the sauce, either offer it separately from the soup or garnish each serving with a generous tablespoonful of it.

ROUILLE
France

Yield: about 1½ cups
Preparation: about 35 minutes

Garlicky and pungent, a sauce with a wallop for fish soups.

1 medium potato, peeled

In the broth of fish soup, cook the potato for 25 minutes, or until it is tender; chop it coarse.

4 large cloves garlic, peeled and chopped coarse
2 pimientos (from a 4-ounce jar)
1 teaspoon thyme
5 tablespoons olive oil

In the container of a food processor or blender, combine the potato and these four ingredients. Whirl them until the mixture is smooth. Transfer it to a mixing bowl.

Few drops of Tabasco sauce
Salt
Pepper

Season the sauce to taste with Tabasco, salt, and pepper.

To serve the sauce, stir into it about 3 tablespoonfuls of hot fish soup. Transfer it to a sauceboat and offer it separately.

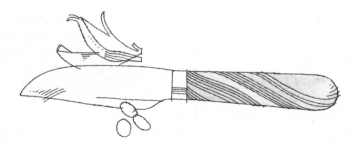

APPENDIX

Basic Soup Stocks

BEEF (BROWN) STOCK

Yield: about 7 cups
Preparation: about 3½ hours

1½ pounds cracked marrow
 bone
 3 pounds lean beef (shin or
 other soup meat), chopped
 coarse
 1 medium-size carrot, scraped
 and chopped
 1 large rib celery, chopped,
 with its leaves
 1 clove garlic, peeled and
 split
 1 medium-size onion, peeled
 and quartered
 1 small white turnip, scraped
 and chopped coarse
 Bouquet garni (with 3
 whole cloves), page 2
 2 teaspoons sugar
1½ teaspoons salt
 8 cups water

In a soup kettle, combine all the ingredients. Bring the liquid to the boil, skimming it as necessary; reduce the heat and simmer the mixture, covered, for 3 hours. Strain it (the beef pieces may be used in some other recipe). Discard the residue. Allow it to cool. Refrigerate it overnight. If desired, clarify the stock, page 247.

CHICKEN STOCK

Yield: about 7 cups
Preparation: about 3½ hours

1 (4-pound) stewing fowl, disjointed
1 medium-size carrot, scraped and chopped
2 ribs celery, chopped, with their leaves
1 medium-size onion, peeled and chopped
   Bouquet garni, page 2
1 teaspoon sugar
1 teaspoon salt
8 cups water

In a soup kettle, combine all the ingredients. Bring the liquid to the boil, reduce the heat, and simmer the mixture, covered, for 2 hours. Strain it (the chicken meat may be used in some other recipe). Discard the residue. Allow it to cool. Refrigerate it overnight. If desired, clarify the stock, page 247.

FISH STOCK

Yield: about 8 cups
Preparation: about 1 hour

2 pounds fish heads, bones, and trimmings of lean fish
1 medium-size carrot, scraped and sliced thin
1 medium-size rib celery, chopped, with its leaves
1 large onion, peeled and chopped
   Bouquet garni, page 2
1 teaspoon sugar
2 teaspoons salt
6 cups water
2 cups dry white wine

In a soup kettle, combine all the ingredients. Bring the liquid to the boil, reduce the heat, and simmer the mixture, uncovered, for 30 minutes. If desired, for a stronger flavor, cook the stock for an additional 15 minutes.
Strain the stock through two or three layers of cheesecloth, discarding the residue. Allow it to cool before refrigerating it. If desired, clarify the stock, page 247.

VEAL (WHITE) STOCK

Yield: about 8 cups
Preparation: about 3½ hours

1 veal knuckle
2 pounds veal bones, if available
3½ pounds shoulder of veal, cubed
2 medium-size carrots, scraped and sliced thin
2 large ribs celery, chopped, with their leaves
2 leeks, rinsed and chopped, the white part only
2 large onions, peeled and chopped
Bouquet garni, page 2
2 teaspoons sugar
2 teaspoons salt
4 quarts water

Tie the veal knuckle and bones in cheesecloth for easy removal from the broth. In a soup kettle, arrange the veal meat, knuckle, and bones. Add the vegetables, *bouquet garni,* sugar, and salt. Add the water.

Bring the liquid to the boil, reduce the heat, and simmer the mixture, covered, for 1 hour. Remove the cover and continue simmering for 2 hours, or until about one half of the liquid has evaporated and the flavor of the broth is full-bodied.

Remove the veal knuckle and bones and *bouquet garni*. Strain the stock, discarding the residue (the cubed meat may be used in another recipe). Allow the stock to cool and then refrigerate it overnight. If desired, clarify the stock, page 247.

VEGETABLE STOCK

Yield: about 8 cups
Preparation: about 2 hours

4 tablespoons butter
2 medium-size carrots, scraped and sliced thin
1 large rib celery, chopped, with its leaves
1 small head lettuce, chopped
3 medium-size onions, peeled and chopped
1 medium-size white turnip, scraped and chopped

In a soup kettle, heat the butter and in it, over gentle heat, cook these five vegetables, covered, for 20 minutes.

2 large ripe tomatoes,
  quartered
2 bay leaves
2 whole cloves
1 clove garlic, peeled and
  sliced lengthwise
8 sprigs parsley
8 peppercorns
½ teaspoon thyme
2 teaspoons sugar
  Salt
8 cups water

To the contents of the soup kettle, add the tomatoes. Tie the herbs and spices loosely in cheesecloth and add them to the kettle. Add the sugar and some salt. Finally, add the water.

Bring the liquid to the boil, reduce the heat, and simmer the vegetables, covered, for 1½ hours. Strain the broth through a fine sieve, discarding the residue. (For clear stock, do not mash the vegetables when straining them. If desired, for substantial, main-dish soups, use a slightly coarser sieve and force the vegetables, except skins and seeds, through it.) Add more salt, if desired, to taste. Allow the stock to cool before storing it in the refrigerator. If desired, clarify the stock; see below.

To Clarify Stock: Unless the soup is to be served clear (with no cloudiness whatsoever), it is not necessary to clarify stock. To do so, however, remove any solidified fat from stock which has been refrigerated overnight. Pour the stock into a large saucepan. To it, add 1 egg white beaten with 2 tablespoonfuls of cold water (use a fork to beat the mixture); add the crushed egg shell, to which sediment in the stock will adhere. Bring the stock to the boil for 2 minutes; reduce the heat to the lowest level and allow the stock to stand without simmering for 20 minutes. Strain the stock through two layers of cheesecloth.

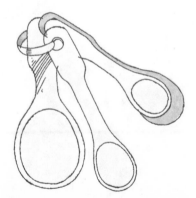

INDEX

Bouquet garni, 2
Bread dumplings, 236
Bread soup, 115
Broccoli soup, cream of, 158
  with garlic, 158
Broth, canned, 2
  to defat, 2
Broth, celery, 116
Brown stock, 244
Burgoo (Kentucky burgoo) (United
    States), 14
Buttermilk soup
  beet and, chilled, 139
  chilled, 139
  lamb and, 24

C
Cabbage soups, 88–90
  cream of, 159
  potato and, 104
Caldo verde (Portugal), 107
Carrot soup, 92
  cream of, 60
    chilled, 198
  orange and, 92
  potato and, 104, 106
  tomato and, 92
  vichyssoise, 145
  yogurt and, chilled, 140
Cauliflower soup, cream of, 162
Celeriac soup, cream of, 163
Celery soup
  broth, 116
  cream of, 164
  leek and, 116
  tomato and, clear, 135
Celery root soup, cream of, 163
Cheddar soup, 208
Cheese
  croutons, 34
  -flavored meatballs, 240
  as garnish, 3
  toasts, 234
Cheese soups, 207–10
  Austrian, 209
  Cheddar, 208
  cheese and corn chowder, 211
  cucumber and, chilled, 212
  Gouda, with vegetable, 215
  leek and, 212

onion and, 213–14
  potato and, 104
  Switzerland, 210
  tomato soup, cream of, with cheese,
    214
  vegetable with Gouda, 215
  winter squash with, 216
Cherry soup, 224–25
  cream of, chilled, 225
Chestnut soup, cream of, 165
Chicken soup
  apple and, cream of, 166
  cream of, curried, 166
  giblet and barley, 44
  gumbo, 39
  ham and, 45
  orange and chicken consommé, 117
  ragout, 40
  tarragon and chicken consommé,
    117
Chicken stock, 245
Chick-pea soup, 64
  chorizo and, 65
  lamb and, 65
  vegetable and, 65
Chilled cream and cream-style soups,
    see Cream and cream-style
    soups, chilled
Chilled thin soups, see Thin soups,
    chilled
Chorizo, chick-pea soup and, 65
Chowder
  cheese and corn, 211
  clam, Manhattan, 57
  clam, New England, 58
  corn, 93
    cheese and, 211
  crab, 59
  dried corn, 94
  fish, 50–52
  lobster, 59
  scallop, 53
  shrimp, 54
Cioppino (United States), 56
Clam
  chowder, Manhattan, 57
  chowder, New England, 58
  cream of spinach and clam soup,
    185
  vichyssoise, 145

ABOUT THE AUTHOR

Robert Ackart has had three careers—first as a teacher of college English, then as an operatic stage director in Europe and America, and now as the author of eight books on food and cooking, among them the Tastemaker Award winning *A Celebration of Vegetables*. He is also an avid gardener and grows many of the ingredients for his recipes at his home in Katonah, New York.

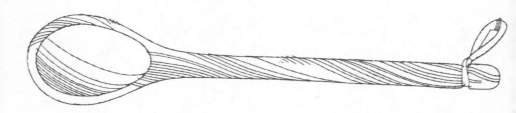